Praise for Robert Garcia

"Congressman Robert Garcia was a trailblazer in public service and a champion for Latino communities in New York and across our nation. I am proud to have called him a friend. He devoted his life to fighting for equality and advocating for his community, and I am eternally grateful for the contributions he made while in public office that continue to inspire each of us."

—*Congressman Adriano de Jesús Espaillat Rodríguez, U.S. Representative for New York's 13th Congressional District, the first Dominican American and first formerly undocumented immigrant to ever serve in Congress.*

MAN OF THE PEOPLE

The Autobiography of Congressman Robert Garcia

Robert Garcia

Arte Público Press
Houston, Texas

Recovering the past, creating the future

Arte Público Press
University of Houston
4902 Gulf Fwy, Bldg 19, Rm 100
Houston, Texas 77204-2004

Cover design by Mora Des¡gn

Front cover, main photo by permission of the NALEO Educational Fund; ©JamesKegley from the NALEO 33rd Annual Conference, 2016.

Library of Congress Control Number: 2023933249

22 23 24   4 3 2 1

To the people of the Bronx . . .
past, present and future.

Table of Contents

Acknowledgements

This autobiography is being published posthumously, and it therefore falls on me to acknowledge those dear people, friends and family who made its writing over the final thirteen years of Bob Garcia's life on Earth the truly rich experience it has been.

Before a word is written, or a thought committed to paper, there needs to be a reason for putting it in writing. Bob was a man of action, on a mission of public service, and it took a while for him to be convinced that he had something worthwhile to say for posterity. He was not one to write lengthy political treatises; he'd rather tell a story of Everyman to inspire subsequent generations to consider Public Service as a noble career. He himself felt this calling was akin to a religious vocation, a sacred calling, and he wanted young people to feel that calling as well.

Throughout his twenty-five years in public life, Bob never missed a graduation in his district and often went beyond those commencements to speak to young people wherever he possibly could. His speech was always along the lines of his own personal story with the clear message: "Don't let anyone tell you that because you came from the Bronx, or because of the color of your skin, you aren't worthy to aspire to lead our Nation! You are as good as anyone else, and this country needs YOU to serve! I did it in spite of the odds . . . and so can you."

Raúl Yzaguirre. Perhaps the person most responsible for convincing Bob to finally get down to writing his story was the pioneering Hispanic civil rights leader Raúl Yzaguirre, founder of the National Council of La Raza (now UnidosUS). In no uncertain terms he told Bob, "Bobby, you simply must write your story for the purpose of historical integrity. If you don't, someone else will, and you will have lost your voice . . . and we need that voice." This was just the push-start that Bob needed after Rudy Giuliani engineered the politically motivated indictment that dragged us both through seven years of degrading publicity and the two trials that ended in both winning our appeals. Raúl was a constant friend, and Bob heeded his good advice; we were both grateful to him. Thank you, dear friend.

Justice Sonia Sotomayor. In another context, the final push to get his book going happened during a small dinner party at a friend's home attended by another Bronxite, the Honorable Justice Sonia Sotomayor, who had recently been appointed to the US Supreme Court. Sitting across from Bob, she leaned forward and told him, "Bob, a lot of the success we have in life depends on being in the right place and at the right time in history. We all stand on someone else's shoulders who opened the door of possibilities for us. You opened doors for me and many others . . . and you need to tell people your story. Please write the book." These were words he took to heart as that very week he committed himself to the task. You, dear friend, were certainly the right person, with the right words, at the right time in the history of this book, and we are forever indebted.

Loretta Phelps de Córdova. The actual task of getting Bob's story on paper (more accurately, on computer) first fell to a friend of mine from early adulthood in Puerto Rico: Loretta Phelps de Córdova, a PhD, author and historian. Loretta had married my schoolmate and then Judge Roberto Córdova and had moved to the island where we became friends. She had eventually moved back to the States and was living in Centerville, a small town near our home in Middleburg, Virginia, where Bob and I were adapting to a kind of retirement from public life. Over the course of several years, Bob would make his notes with care at home and then, several times a week, would drive to her home, where he spent a good part of the mornings or afternoons with her. Without your expert guidance, Loretta, there would be, simply put, no book. Thank you for your professional dedication and friendship; you, too, were certainly the right person, there at the right time in history, for us.

Bob's doctors. By November of 2012, it had become apparent that Bob's health was in decline. His medical team at George Washington University Hospital—Dr. Charles Faselis, head of internal medicine, and Dr. Guillermo Gutiérrez, head of the department of pulmonology, met with us and strongly recommended we move from Virginia to a warm climate as soon as possible to give Bob the best quality of life. Over the Christmas holidays, we decided to go to Puerto Rico for several weeks to take a break from the cold and damp weather. Bob's breathing noticeably improved immediately after arriving, leading us to make the commitment to move as soon as possible and make Puerto Rico our new home.

When we returned to Virginia, we began downsizing and packing up a big house to fit into an apartment. Both Dr. Faselis and Dr. Gutiérrez were invaluable in setting up his medical care with a strong team at the Veterans Hospital in Puerto Rico. Dr. Gutiérrez collaborated with the Head of Pulmonary Care Dr. Hiram Rodríguez and Dr. Juan Carlos Martínez González, who took over as his internal medicine doctor. The personal attention and excellent VA facilities on the island literally kept Bob going until the latter part of 2016, when he was admitted for his final hospitalization in December, passing on January 25, 2017, two weeks after his 84th birthday. Thank you all for your kind care and friendship over those final years. Without you, there would have been only the shadow of Bob's story, as it was in those last five years you made possible that he personally reworked and added to this autobiography.

Ron Rosenberg and Patricia Molther-Rosenberg. Even before moving to Puerto Rico we both already had many friends, and even some family, with whom we had kept in touch with over the years. In fact, one of my best friends on earth, Patricia and her husband, Ron, were instrumental in helping us find our wonderful new home in the same building they lived in, the Torre de la Reina condominium. The salt air breeze from the Atlantic Ocean and Muñoz Rivera Park across from El Escambrón Beach in San Juan was an ideal location; we were able to rent one of the building's several penthouses . . . and with an open-ended lease! The large open terrace (we installed a flagpole and flew the Stars and Stripes 24/7) became our favorite site for working on the book. It felt like home, and having Pat close by was very comforting, as she was a source of encouragement in flagging moments. Thank you both for your friendship and encouraging support.

Manny Casiano. Another key to Bob successfully focusing on the task at hand was Manny's invitation for Bob to share an office at San Juan-based Casiano Communications, the largest US Hispanic-owned publisher of magazines and periodicals in the United States, which had started out as one of the very first area business publications in 1975 and was the region's weekly "business bible" for forty-three years: *Caribbean Business*. The company's founder, CEO and publisher, Manuel "Manny" Casiano, was a longtime friend of Bob's going back to their early years in New York. Following the sale of his successful, bi-coastal, special-effects film company—he had won several technical Emmy Awards—Manny and his wife Nora had moved to Puerto Rico in the early 1970s at the invitation of industrialist and then Governor of Puerto Rico, Don Luis A. Ferré, who appointed him to head Fomento, the island's agency in charge of promoting job creation. For a man like Bob, now retired, it was a great feeling to put on a suit and tie several times a week and "go to the office." It helped get his brain in gear! Thank you, Manny and Nora, for your unwavering faith in Bob, as well as your tangible help and friendship over the years. It was at Casiano Communications that Bob met the person who pulled the whole book together and helped Bob organize it into a readable story . . . the confluence of yet another "someone being in the right place at the right time."

Nicholas Karahalios. With a wealth of experience in economic development, marketing and media, Chicago native Nicholas Karahalios had been working for Manny as a marketing expert on various occasions since 1985. He is also an excellent wordsmith and helped greatly by reorganizing and editing the original manuscript for publication. Nick became a dear friend and is to this day serving as secretary of the non-profit "Congressman Robert Garcia Legacy Fund." I am personally most grateful for his past and continuing work in promoting Bob's autobiography as well as taking it to the next level as a documentary film, which will follow as another facet of Bob's legacy project. Bob and Nick spent many hours in their shared office at Casiano Communications. So I was not surprised when, among the final instructions Bob gave me in the last few weeks before his passing, he said: "Jane, stay close to Nick, you can trust him. He is very smart"—something I've never had cause to doubt.

Governor Bill Richardson. One of the beneficiaries of the work and vision of Bob Garcia's accomplishments in connection with the 1980 census was that it soon doubled the number of Hispanics in Congress, up from the four that had then made up the newly formed Congressional Hispanic Caucus (CHC), of which Bob was a member. Four new Hispanics were elected, among them Bill Richardson of New Mexico. Bill caught Bob's attention and he immediately prevailed on Bill to take over as chairman of the CHC Institute, a position that Bob had chaired for almost four years. That prompted a tongue-in-cheek rebuke from Bob's closest friend in Congress and part of the New York Delegation, Charlie Rangel. "Hey, Bob, what are you? Crazy? You don't make a new freshman a chair of anything! He hasn't paid his dues here yet!" To which Bob responded, "But he's really very smart, Charlie!" Bill quickly proved Bob right, going on to be elected governor of New Mexico and appointed ambassador to the United Nations, as well as special envoy and the successful mediator in the release of American hostages in many parts of the world. Thank you, Bill, for the friendship and unwavering faith you and Barb always had during our darkest days. Thank you as well for your eloquent words dedicated to Bob in your gracious "Prologue" to this book. You knew his worth, understood his vision and were always ready to help Bob. I am proud to count you as a dear friend.

Dr. Félix Matos. When Bob decided to resign from his congressional seat in 1990, he arranged to leave the official papers from his entire twenty-five years in public service—from the NY State Assembly and Senate as well as Congress—to Hunter College, part of the CUNY System. The reasoning was that there was already the nucleus of a dedicated Centro de Estudios Puertorriqueños, and he was, after all, a proud Puerto Rican New Yorker (Nuyorican). It felt natural and Dr. Félix Matos, Chancellor of CUNY, was instrumental in reaching this decision and facilitating the process. Most recently, Dr. Matos was the direct link to the University of Houston's Arte Público Press, which is publishing this book, and to its director, Dr. Nicolás Kanellos. Thank you, dear Felo, for your firm belief that Bob's story needed to be published for future generations and for going out of your way to help make it happen.

Roberto Sancho. Nothing happens without money. The vehicle to facilitate the publication and dissemination of Bob's inspiring story and legacy to students, as well as to ultimately provide scholarships to those pursuing a career in public policy, was the creation of the non-profit Congressman Robert Garcia Legacy Fund. Its advisory board is a reflection of the many friends who supported and loved Bob in his life and career over the years. While all have been active contributors to the legacy project's ongoing existence, I do need to single out Roberto Sancho of Bronx Lebanon Hospital for its continuing support and generous donations over the past four years, giving us the operating funds to get things done. Thank you, Bob, for all the help that allowed us to get the book edited for publication as well as to undertake the first efforts toward the documentary film.

Finally, to our blended family, I add my heartfelt thanks to those in Bob's "Preface." To all our children for just being there for us both during all these years. As his heirs, in many ways you were always his true motivation! God bless you all.

Jane Lee Garcia
President
Congressman Robert Garcia Legacy Fund, Inc.

Prologue

Bob Garcia's memoir reflects a life of struggle and achievement. His kind of leadership grew and was tested first in the poor, rough streets of the South Bronx and then in the cold, muddy fields of Korea, before arriving at the New York Senate and the US House of Representatives.

This work traces his youth and manhood in details we can marvel at. His community ties together the island of Puerto Rico and the City of New York into what Bob proudly calls his Nuyorican heritage. His father works hard at his job and weekends at a storefront church. His mother saves their small income to buy Easter clothes and is savvy enough to run her hand over her teenage son's arms as a hug, making sure there are no needle tracks in those days of drugs and violence in the neighborhood. She signs the consent for him to volunteer for the US Army when he is only seventeen years old. In distant Korea, he shivers in combat and vows to become a pastor like his sister, should he live. He returns to the brilliant lights of Broadway and the enticing chance to study with the GI Bill, get a good job and go places in the world.

The young man works, marries and starts a family, while beginning politics in the very best way: at ground level, person to person. Bob enters the civil rights movement with an energy and commitment to the cause, up and down the tenement stairs, garnering votes for John F. Kennedy in the Democratic Convention, talking and listening to the populace and then bursting into the limelight as he's chosen to run on the Democratic ticket for the New York Assembly.

From there to minority leader (Democrat) in the New York Senate, learning the intricate unwritten and written rules of negotiating and legislating, Bob continually grows in stature. By now he is a beloved figure in the South Bronx and an adept practitioner of the difficult art of politics. Everyone in Albany and the City of New York seems to know and respect him. His official presence at the Attica prison riots moves him to work further at prisoner rehabilitation.

His rise to national Hispanic leadership mirrors the incredible feat of gaining his seat to Congress in the teeth of entrenched control of a Democratic borough boss, who puts his own favorite on the party ticket. Shockingly, the Republicans allow him to run on their side, and Bob overthrows the will of the boss, gains the votes of the electorate and goes on to join the Democratic caucus in Congress. I don't think that has been done before.

Once in Congress, he immediately surges to leadership, skillfully using the US Census and various committees to lead the charge for the Black and Hispanic Caucus, bringing it into the twentieth century. He works hard for civil rights, not only in his own country, but at the international level.

More than a decade later, suffering an indictment and then winning appellate court exoneration, Bob retires from Congress and continues forward in the community. The caucus grows at many levels, always supported by Bob. Forty years later, the Congressional Hispanic Coalition Institute (CHCI) is now a non-partisan, non-profit organization, an effective powerhouse to provide congressional internships and stimulate Hispanic participation in civic life.

Bob and his wife Jane (whose dynamic presence in the Hispanic cultural scene is well known) receive plaudits from the CHCI. He continues work in congressional relations and Christian Fellowship.

My mother was Mexican and my father American, so I grew up with a different kind of bicultural background. When I first met Bob, I was beginning my own electoral story. He had crisscrossed the country, including Puerto Rico, holding dozens of hearings to promote Hispanic participation in the 1980 census. That work directly influenced the redistricting of congressional representation and gave

New Mexico another position in the House of Representatives. I won it.

As a much-respected congressman, Bob helped me on many issues as I was getting my feet wet. In the midst of some turmoil, Bob drafted me to take his place as leader of the burgeoning Hispanic Caucus in Congress, which, thanks to him, was cooperating with the Blacks in the House. I continued my work in government at high levels, including cabinet positions and, most recently, as governor of New Mexico. I know first-hand the galvanizing importance of Bob Garcia.

I agree with Supreme Court Justice Sonia Sotomayor, another and younger distinguished citizen from the Bronx, who told him, "You must tell your story, Bobby. You are one of the reasons I'm here today. You've been a pioneer for my generation."

Here's his story, ably told by Bob himself. . . .

Read it!

Bill Richardson
Governor of New Mexico 2003-2011
Former US Ambassador to the United Nations
Former US Secretary of Energy during the Clinton Administration

September 25, 2018

Preface

Each person has his own tale. This is mine. I want to share my story here: what I owe to my beloved country, the United States, with all its promise and pitfalls, its extraordinary and enduring reality of a living Bill of Rights. To my old neighborhood, the South Bronx, crowded tenements and vital, tough, loving people. To the island my parents called home, Puerto Rico, lush, green and beautiful, struggling with poverty and a colonial sense of inferiority, while harboring a traditional greatness of heart. And to my family, my first wife Anita Medina, who, like me, was a product of the South Bronx in the 1940s and '50s, who gave me my two sons Robert William and Kenneth Ralph, and my adopted daughter Rosalind. To Jane, my wife of thirty-six years and the four children that came into my life with her: Edward, Robert and Caroline Power and Kirsten Marie Matos. We surely don't make our paths alone.

Looking back at my life, I realize how deeply I am my father's son. His honesty and passion to help others, to bring people together, to follow Christ's path . . . those qualities I've tried to make my own. Of course, I have my own zest for life. All these together have driven me to my life's work to seek equality for those less blessed by fortune, while seeking my personal happiness and success in the world. When I first ran for the New York State Assembly, under the original Voting Rights Act passed in 1964, it was a time when all minority groups were seeking equality and political empowerment. I am proud to have been one of the leaders who pioneered this movement and helped lead the way for those who came after me.

In the electoral year of 2012, we Hispanics made our mark both as voters and leaders in the community. Let me tell you how this poor Nuyorican (New York Puerto Rican) kid, now a man who's old in age and young at heart, has seen the mountains and the valleys of experience and has had a wonderful time through it all.

This isn't a sociological dissertation, to be sure. I do however want to share with the reader a story of my life of struggle and faith and joy throughout bad and good times. I am delighted to have represented my beloved South Bronx in the extraordinary and challenging world of the New York Legislature and the US Congress. From learning how to hustle on the street with stickball, I had to learn how to hustle in the give-and-take of the Republican-dominated state legislature and then in the Democratic caucuses in the US House of Representatives. In NATO I rubbed shoulders with world leaders and helped make policy decisions. I learned to listen to the other guy, to give an honest opinion with discretion and leadership. It's always about making your word your bond.

This is also a story reflecting my Puerto Rican roots and seeing the changes and challenges of both my ancestral island and my own United States, my love for all things Hispanic, my special appreciation for people of color, my exuberant enthusiasm for sharing with others of all backgrounds, my deep interest in observing and analyzing politics and being involved in policy making while undoubtedly enjoying the so-called "good life" of what the material world can offer. Underlying all this is a bedrock belief in the Christian God and the transformational power of Jesus Christ in our daily lives, as well as my passion to measure up to what Christ demands of me on a daily basis. It's always a challenge.

CHAPTER ONE
My Puerto Rican Roots

My dad's father was a Spanish soldier from Álava in the northern Basque region of Spain who was stationed in what was then Spain's colony in the Caribbean: Puerto Rico. Like so many of his fellow Spaniards, he fled to hide in the mountains when the Americans invaded the island in 1898 during the Spanish-American War. He eventually ended up in the town of Coamo, Puerto Rico, not too far from the biggest city on the southern coast and its center of commerce, Ponce. I remember his mother, who visited us when I was a child in New York, as a dark-skinned and wrinkled old woman with straight black hair. She made me think of the island's Taíno indians, smoking her little cigar and looking at me with intense dark black eyes. She radiated heart. It's funny how childhood impressions stamp the memory and don't necessarily capture what the world considers to be reality. Just recently I saw a picture of my grandmother with my parents and me, and she doesn't look that way at all. She's just a well-dressed, white-skinned, serious middle-aged lady. Where was that dark-skinned Taíno matriarch that I remembered? Where had she gone? It makes me wonder about all our memories. . . .

My dad, Rafael, whose Garcia-González surname reflected both his father's and mother's lineage in the Puerto Rican and Spanish style, was born and grew up in the green-hilled town of Coamo. It was, and still is, a farming and cattle area, but also a kind of local resort due to its hot springs and a natural spa. My father had four siblings: Pablo (my godfather), Sixto, Rufina and Suncha. By the way,

1

the island's governor elected in 2012 is a García (Alejandro García Padilla), from Coamo too, and some of my family claim kinship. Be that as it may, everyone in Puerto Rico seems to be related somehow: a cousin of a cousin or next-door neighbor of a great aunt or something of the sort.

My father got a job at the Central Aguirre, a huge sugarcane mill on the southern coast between Guayama and Ponce. Sugar cultivation, controlled by local and stateside monopolies, drove the island's economy in those days. "King Sugar" they called it. Although once regarded as producing the coffee "of kings and popes," coffee plantations in the mountains had suffered from a series of hurricanes. Sugar, and rum distilled from sugar molasses, picked up the slack while the low-paid, hard-worked cane cutters, not unlike cotton pickers in the South, brought in the coastal cash crop. Many of the companies that owned the mills were headquartered in New England.

My dad's job wasn't great, but he was fortunate to have it. I don't know exactly what he did in the mill, but he told us that at least he didn't have to wield a machete to cut cane in the densely planted, rat-infested fields, like his brother Pablo. In the mill, they ground and pressed the cut cane stalks to produce sugar, molasses and bagasse. Dad told us later that he'd walk back and forth to his home in Coamo on the weekends with food from the company store for his mother. It was a journey of many miles between the coast and the foothills. He was healthy and strong, despite the prevalence of parasitical anemia and tropical diseases. Just eating enough and surviving was hard, but he managed.

My mom, Rosa Rodríguez Roche, was born on the south coast in the poor neighborhood of La Playa de Ponce. It was, and still is, a low-lying swampy area facing the Caribbean Sea. By now the contaminated waters of the mangroves have been fairly well cleaned up, but it was polluted for many years and filled with shacks. Mom's parents died when she was young, and their sweet, lovely dark-eyed girl and her sisters were brought up by various relatives in La Playa, where each family was poorer than the next. She sometimes didn't know where she'd be sleeping at night, as she was moved from one family to the next, and that kind of upbringing gave her a lifelong feeling of insecurity. In spite of that unsettled upbringing, her sisters were good to her, and she grew into a kind, good woman who became a loving wife and mother. Even so, she was subject to occasional bouts of depression. She leaned on my older sister Aimee, who always had an inner strength that fortified our whole family.

Many years later, I would spend the night at my maternal aunt Estefanía's little wooden house there on Guadalupe Street in La Playa de Ponce, just down the street from the convent of my friend Sor Isolina Ferré, daughter of a wealthy Ponce family and sister of industrialist and future governor Luis A. Ferré. Sister Isolina became a caring godmother to the Puerto Ricans in the South Bronx and later returned to her native city, where she founded a world-renowned community center for the poor. Another neighbor born on the same street was a poor but strong boy called José "Chegui" Torres, who became a light heavyweight champion boxer.

The first time I slept in that Playa neighborhood of little houses, shanties and mangroves, it was under a mosquito net and, believe me, the protection was really needed! Imagine how it must have been in my mother's day, with mosquitoes out of control spreading malaria among the tuberculosis-ridden poor. I think of my mother's childhood in those harsh conditions and am happy that she was able to have a comfortable old age as a widow living with Aimee in Rockland County, north of New York City, and that she'd also had the chance to own her own home in the Santa Monica neighborhood of Bayamón, close to the capital city of San Juan.

How did my parents, those poor young people who hardly spoke English, ever get it together and find the courage to set off for New York? They had only a few years of public school, no money and no job prospects on the mainland. It took audacity and bravery to leave for the unknown. How I admire them . . . and all who have dared to begin their lives anew in the United States!

CHAPTER TWO

Growing Up in the South Bronx

Immigrants made up the South Bronx, just as they make up, and have always made up, the whole United States going back to colonial times. My parents had joined their fellow Puerto Ricans in 1924—seven years after the US government granted American citizenship to all Puerto Ricans—as part of the South Bronx stew: Eastern European Jews, Blacks, Greeks, Italians and Irish. Yes, it was the proverbial melting pot. Just a handful of Puerto Ricans and Spanish-speakers lived there then, so most of my friends came out of that stew. Back then there were no "Puerto Ricans," "Ricans" or "Spics" used as labels. We were simply referred to as "Spanish."

Looking back, the date of my dad's arrival was significant if not on purpose: July 4, 1924. Jobs were plentiful in the US post-World War I economy, and he quickly found steady work as a polisher/buffer for a high-end lamp maker, Caldwell Shops, in Manhattan. Caldwell provided lighting for the mansions of New York's new millionaires, Saint Patrick's Cathedral, the New York Public Library and scores of other private and public institutions throughout the city and the nation, including the White House. My dad, Rafael, made friends easily and settled in. My mom, Rosa, lived with relatives and she most probably worked for a while until she married. My parents had arrived in New York City from Puerto Rico separately in 1924; they hadn't known each other on the island. And while they didn't have to go through Ellis Island because they were already US citizens, I'm sure New York felt like a foreign land to them. I visualize them as

4

urban pioneers in the Promised Land. Both had the zest of youth, the desire to succeed and a belief in the "American Dream."

My story begins, thus, as do so many stories in the United States, with a family that endured poverty and struggle, surviving with a hard-work ethic and the bedrock of faith. We moved around within the same neighborhood. Sometimes it was living in a basement apartment where Dad got a good deal serving as the resident janitor for the building, in addition to his regular job. The apartment was always small and always clean, with a few little pictures, including one of Franklin Delano Roosevelt, on the wall. It was cold in the winter and hot in the summer.

My parents were married in 1926 in the Methodist Church on Park Avenue in Spanish Harlem. They soon started a family. First came my brother Ralph, then my two sisters Aimee and Estelle, and I was the *bebé*. My dad, from beginning to end, was always a model of stability in an environment of struggle and want. My mom was always at home, cooking, sewing, cleaning, keeping the family accounts and caring for us kids.

Dad held his job with Caldwell all through the Depression and for forty years beyond. He proudly belonged to the Electrical Workers' Union, which inspired my lifelong loyalty to organized labor. He'd leave at seven o'clock each morning to catch the IRT subway at 138th and Brook Avenue with a cup of coffee in his hand. For lunch he'd buy a quart of milk and a sandwich. All that for $5 a week! My mother kept the family books, and that was the food allowance she assigned him.

Dad was always kind, not only to his family but to outsiders as well. One of his more common heartfelt phrases when greeting a friend or stranger was, "*su servidor*," meaning "your servant," a common, polite expression in Puerto Rico and still much used. But rather than a perfunctory statement, Dad actually meant it. He always inspired me with his dignity, gentleness and work ethic. He never missed a day of work. (My mother told me she'd checked him out before agreeing to marry him, tempting him to see if he was really as stable as he appeared, by asking him to go off to the park for a picnic on a workday, but he never succumbed.)

As I said earlier, Mother had been an orphan in Puerto Rico, bouncing from relative to relative from a young age, and therefore stability was the most important thing in her life, as well as an endearing quality in a man. Her testing my father for that quality was not frivolous but a deep-rooted need. The first home I remember was the tenement at 173 Brook Avenue, a five-story walk-up with twenty apartments. Just like in their towns and villages in Puerto Rico, everybody not only knew everybody else, but they also knew everybody else's business. Few secrets were kept that didn't make the rounds of gossip in the building, sometimes spilling out into the neighborhood. Each window facing the street had an old pillow over the sill, where the women would lean out to call to their kids in the street, to the street vendors or to one another. That was their "neighborhood watch," and we kids knew there would be hell to pay if any of those mothers called out a reprimand and we didn't obey. Whether it was our own mother or someone else's, it meant serious business, especially if one of them said, "I'm going to tell your mother!" That would be BIG trouble. We learned to respect our elders because they relied on each other to raise us. It was truly an urban village. Dinnertime was a chorus of boys' names called out from the windows, each boy knowing his own mother's call no matter how many had the same name. Mine was "Bo-o-obbbeeee." And it didn't matter if it came as I was finally getting my long-awaited turn at bat in the daily street stickball game. I would drop everything and run home like a bullet.

Walking upstairs to our apartment around lunch or dinnertime was like walking through the League of Nations—this was before the United Nations—of delicious and exotic aromas. By the time I got to our place, I had smelled savory lamb stew, Irish corned beef and cabbage, simmering Italian pasta sauce and exotic Greek food, along with the other cooking coming from every floor. By the time I got to our apartment, I was drooling.

A growing boy, and already with big hands and feet, I knew I'd become a big man . . . if only I could eat enough. I was always hungry. Today, my wife Jane says that's why we have the pantry overflowing . . . that I'm still secretly afraid we won't have enough to eat. She's probably right; old habits die hard!

We'd all crowd expectantly around the dinner table: Dad, Mom, Ralph, Aimee, Estelle and me. Despite my dad's being a consistent provider, with my wanting to attain my destined height, I would often pipe up with a plaintive plea: "Mom, can't we have something else? It's always the same thing, and I'm still hungry." Sometimes it was *funche* (cornmeal, sort of a Puerto Rican polenta) three times a day: for breakfast, for lunch and for dinner. My mother would boil it up with a little salt or sugar, and there it was in the bowl: our meal. It was not one that I especially relished after the tempting savory smells beckoning me from the other apartments.

"Bobby, fill up on the *funche*! It's all we can afford until your father's next paycheck. Be happy with that!"

My mother didn't feel sorry for me, and she just called it the way it was . . . not angry, but matter of fact, knowing she had saved and stretched every penny to feed and clothe her growing family.

My sister Aimee, always the peacemaker and my self-appointed guardian, would chime in with her persuasive, firm voice. "Don't worry about it, Bobby, just eat! Think of all the poor souls who have nothing. At least we have a roof over our heads and parents who care for us. Thank God for both!"

I can't romanticize it. We did suffer cold and hunger, but how I loved it when my mother had the extra money to cook her delicious rice and beans and *tostones* (green plantain fritters) or my all-time favorites, *arroz con pollo* (chicken and rice) or sweet plantain and meat-filled *piñón* instead of the dreaded *funche*!

What I recall, above all, was a free and happy childhood full of love and a sense of family. And our neat neighborhood had a sense of history. In nearby St. Ann's Episcopal Church on St. Ann's Avenue, where else?—stands the tomb of an actual signer of the Declaration of Independence, Governor Lewis Morris, born in what we know today as the Morrisania section of the Bronx, first settled by the Dutch and named after Jonas Bronck (c. 1600-1643). Morris wrote much of the US Constitution, and it always struck me, even as a boy, that he was buried right there in our own South Bronx. That somehow gave us what we call today "added value."

Because everything is truly relative, we didn't even know we were considered poor because all our neighbors were in the same boat. In the thirties and forties, when I was a boy, the South Bronx was a poor, but safe, working-class neighborhood. This was before the horrible plague of drugs hit the streets. We played on car-less streets and went to Public School 43 around the corner. As a boy, the freedom to roam the streets of New York was positively breath-taking. I knew all the nooks and crannies of our part of the city like the back of my hand; it was a wonderful primer for a later life in politics. There were not many cars yet—neither we nor those we knew could afford them—and, of course, no malls as we know them today. We had, instead, street-level stores and vendors, and shopping was done locally on a daily basis. The produce wholesalers were located up and down Brook Avenue, where we lived. In the early morning, horse-drawn carts would line up head-to-tail for the loading of their wagons with the fresh produce they would hawk to housewives all around the Bronx. I loved getting up at the crack of dawn to watch the Eastern European Jews keeping up with the demand from all these carts in a constant back and forth of price-haggling, mostly in Yiddish.

Our group of boys was a mix of Irish, Jews, Greeks, Italians and me. We never thought any of us was less than the other, or socially different or inferior. We were just kids together. Without television or money to go to the movies, we made up games and even made our own toys and equipment for our games. During the summers we would make exotic excursions to the "island": the sands of Orchard Beach in the North Bronx. We "explored" construction sites and watched the workmen knock down buildings along the route that would become the Major Degan Expressway, connecting the new Triboro Bridge to the Bronx—the toll was an outrageous 25 cents!

A *New York World Telegram* report in the 1950s described our neighborhood, Mott Haven, as a place filled with "solid, grim, five-story tenements, facing equally grimy five-story tenements . . . people thick as flies on the fire escapes. Every window was crowded with men, women and children and the sidewalks were thronged."

Yep, I was one of that "throng," but it wasn't all that bad. . . . It was my home! We wandered all over and had a good time doing it. It was that way for all the kids. We had fun. Maybe we didn't eat a lot—no junk food, that's for sure—and often we did go hungry. It just made us appreciate the food set out for birthdays and holidays that much more.

I knew each "mom and pop" store, tailor and *bodega* that stretched from 133rd to 138th streets; that was before the high-rise public housing went up. I whizzed through those streets on my roller skates, greeting people on the way.

"Hey, Jerry, give me a pastrami on rye, heavy on the mustard."

"Do ya' have the money, kid? It ain't for free!"

I'd slap a half dollar on his counter for a Coke and the sandwich, and the old guy would always make a wisecrack. I really loved those Jewish delis.

What I remember best about growing up in the South Bronx was that in those days there were not many cars on the street, and the few people who owned automobiles were people that we knew. If we wanted to play stickball in the street, we would go to their homes and ask them to please move their cars. Most of the time they were kind enough to comply. Maybe it had something to do with their car's safety. . . . Who knows, right?

Stickball was the game of choice in those days because it was the one thing we could afford. All we needed was an old broomstick and a red, three-cent Spalding ball. We could play from eight o'clock in the morning until three or four in the afternoon—truly a wonderful day in the life of a young boy. On Sunday afternoons (after church) during the spring, playing stickball was king in the South Bronx. I played on "the Archers," and we'd wait for a team from a nearby neighborhood to come by and challenge us. We Archers would accept the challenge and bet them that we would win. What made us feel even more important was there would be several hundred people from the neighborhood watching, many from their pillowed windowsills.

Another vivid memory is the trolleys. I remember the trolley cars that used to run on St. Ann's Avenue from Bruckner Boulevard and 134th St. to 163rd St. and Third Avenue, as well as the ones that ran up and down 138th Street and those that ran along Willis Avenue and the ones that ran across 149th Street from one end of 149th St. in the Bronx all the way over to Harlem. Then, slowly but surely, the rails in the streets were paved over, and buses started replacing the trolleys—all this transportation available for the very, very expensive price of a nickel in the late 1940s.

And then of course there was the 3rd Avenue "El" (elevated train), which ran from Fordham Road in the Bronx, under the East River and all the way to the Battery in Lower Manhattan. The "El" ran right through the streets of the South Bronx, where public housing now exists: from Third Avenue and 149th St. down to Bruckner Boulevard across the East River and then straight south on Third Avenue into Manhattan.

One very vivid memory is what happened on December 7, 1941. I was playing stickball with the guys on our street, and all of a sudden one of our Greek friends, Mike Noteritis, came running out of our building; he lived on the fourth floor. As he got nearer, we could finally make out what he'd been yelling: "It's war! The Japs bombed Pearl Harbor!"

I had no idea what or where Pearl Harbor was, but even at the age of eight I did understand that war was a bad thing. The next day, December 8, was equally memorable when our principal at P.S. 43 assembled the entire student body to hear President Roosevelt give his "Day of Infamy" speech over the vacuum-tube radio. Years later, in public life, I tried without success to get the name of that principal, since I couldn't remember it after so many years. I just wanted to thank him for his thoughtfulness in including us all in that historic moment.

Our family was directly affected a few years later when my older brother Ralph joined the Army after he turned eighteen. Thankfully, he was one of the WWII soldiers who came home; nearly 420,000 did not.

During the war years, we would have Civil Defense-imposed blackouts and neighborhood training against potential air raids. For us young kids, those were very eerie goings-on, and the only thing we could really see was the air raid warden, usually a familiar figure from the neighborhood. Exterior lights were turned off and window shades drawn. This and other such training made us feel like we were doing our part in the war effort.

We were God-fearing people but not that concerned with religion when I was young. We kids were sent off to Sunday School, and I daresay that was the only moment when my parents were able to be together alone. It was hit or miss: sometimes we went, sometimes not. But then things began to change. I'll never forget an early moment when I thought about God and, in a sense, I brought religion to our family. I must have been about seven years old, throwing a ball on the stoop of our apartment at 173 Brook Avenue early one Sunday morning. As I played there, a lady I knew as Rosita López walked over to me. She was a big woman, kind of moon-faced, with a nice manner. I'd seen her around, always trying to convince people to go to church.

"*Muchachito*," she said, "*¿quieres ir a la iglesia?*" (Little boy, do you want to go to church?)

I thought that would be okay but asked her to go talk to my mother.

So upstairs she went, and the next thing I knew, I was trotting off with the woman to a little Pentecostal storefront church on 136th Street between Brook and St. Ann's Avenue.

Rosita's husband Manuel López was the pastor and founder of the Thessalonica Christian Church. They were really committed Christians. First Mom, then Dad, began attending this church, which led them to become and remain members for the next thirty years! My father became a deacon in the church and was finally asked to become pastor; it would become a major part of his life. First, my father would hand out religious tracts on the street on weekends and, next, he would preach outdoors. It really embarrassed me. And as I sat all those years with my mother and brother and sisters in my dad's church, I never once raised my hand to give myself to the Lord, which was a significant part in their rite. That would have been hypocritical of me. I didn't want to give up my freedom. The Hispanic Pentecostal Church at the time seemed very legalistic to me, with difficult rules and regulations. No fun, for sure! Everything fun was forbidden: dancing, parties, movies. . . . How could you meet girls if you didn't go dancing? I wasn't a very good dancer at first, but I sure loved the mambo and the cha-cha, and the girls' lessons eventually took hold after suffering my clumsiness.

To the Pentecostals, movies were a sin, too. I remember vividly the fear that overcame me sitting in a movie house once with some friends, watching a Roy Rogers movie at the Osceola Theatre on St. Ann's Avenue. Suddenly, I jumped up in fear and ran outside. I ran all the way home because I was sure that God had come in "the Rapture" and taken my family, leaving me behind. It was all very confusing. I saw a God of fear rather than a God of love. As a man now, I see things in a very different way. Back then, I believed that God would help me eventually, but I still couldn't figure out what my role was. I was sure of one thing, though, that if I did give myself to the Lord, God would make me give up all the things I wanted to enjoy, things I was just discovering in my young life.

"Nope, not me, God! Not yet!"

By the time I was a teenager, I was just barely strong enough morally to counter the attraction of another kind of freedom, the rebellious one that pushes you to join a gang and run wild in the streets. All my friends had that same temptation. I sometimes hung out with Jewish and Irish kids in the neighborhood and thought nothing of it; that was well before the huge migration of Puerto Ricans after World War II.

One day the Irish kids from my neighborhood asked me to go with them down to the docks, and they all jumped down to swim and horse around in the water. I didn't join them because I couldn't swim, and it was deep. I just stood there and watched. Suddenly, I saw a bunch of Irish toughs from another neighborhood approaching. I knew they were ready to throw me in and I also knew I'd drown. I was scared to the bone. So, I turned around and went walking . . . cool . . . in the other direction. A teenage boy really had to be alert to prosper in that environment.

On another occasion, my older brother Ralph was cornered by a gang of tough Irish kids, but one of them yelled, "Hey, leave him alone! He's the brother of Bobby Garcia, the one who plays stick-ball. He's okay." Sports ability counted as your "bona fide" in those days.

One day, during summer recess, we went down into the subway station to feed illegal slugs into a penny gum machine. It was exciting to break the law, to defy authority! Unfortunately, a policeman saw us. Three of the group ran away, but the policeman was able to nab Marty Batlon and me.

"Hey, you kids, what ya think ya doin'? Yous are under arrest!" he announced as he clamped a big hand on each of us.

We were taken to the Hecksher Children's Shelter on 105th and 5th Avenue, and our parents were sent for. A police car stopped in front of our apartment, and everyone was alerted to come out and see who was in trouble. The whole Garcia family was disgraced!

The next thing I knew, we were in front of a judge, and my father was there.

The judge asked my dad, "Well, what do think of this, Mr. Garcia? What should we do?"

Dad answered, "Whatever you think is right, Your Honor. He did wrong."

So much for pleading on my behalf!

They threw me in a cell in the juvenile detention center with three other boys for one night. I didn't sleep a wink, scared of my fellow cellmates, and I just kept thinking, "This is horrible. I will never go through something like this again!"

The next day, I was allowed to go home in the custody of my father. He disciplined me by confining me to our apartment for a week. The worse thing was the knowledge that I'd brought shame on our family and disappointed him. That scary incident helped me straighten out and ended my short gang career. I was young, in the sixth grade.

After World War II, just as I was entering my teenage years, things had begun to change in our neighborhood . . . drastically. At that time, hundreds of thousands of landless, poorly educated farm-workers from Puerto Rico were taking the plane to New York, looking for opportunities. The island's agricultural economy of sugar and tobacco just didn't have the jobs and infrastructure to support them. The Puerto Rican government under Governor Luis Muñoz Marín helped send them to the continent in a desperate and complex experiment in social engineering and relocation: as migrant workers in farms throughout the northeast corridor of the United States. But many more came on their own and sought factory work from New York to New Jersey and Massachusetts. At the very same time, drugs were pouring into the South Bronx. The mix of extreme poverty, cultural disorientation and pervasive drugs radically changed our relatively crime-free neighborhood. Suddenly, violence and crime was threatening everyone. Fortunately, my earlier happy childhood on those same streets gave me the strength I needed to survive.

* * *

When I turned fourteen years old, I applied for my working papers in New York State, because in 1947 any person fourteen years or older could legally work until six in the evening. Once I received my working papers, I immediately went to Yankee Stadium to apply for a job selling peanuts and scorecards during baseball games at both Yankee Stadium and the Polo Grounds, the home of the New York Giants (now the San Francisco Giants). When the Yankees were in town, the Giants were on the road and vice versa, so that there was always work.

Back then, games were played only during the day; there were no lights and no night games. I got the job and was able to work just about every day and was done before 6 p.m. In the morning, a bunch of us would wait outside the gate, hoping to be selected to work that day. We worked on 10% commission. Peanuts sold for 10 cents a bag, soda pop was 10 cents a bottle and ice cream was 10 cents a bar, so I'd make one cent selling each. I would sell anywhere from 600 to 700 bags of peanuts a day and would therefore earn between six and seven dollars, which in the late 1940s was really a great deal of money.

As a lover of the game of baseball, I got to see some truly great games and equally great players. I remember seeing Joe DiMaggio in the 1947 World Series and Yogi Berra when he first came up as a catcher for the Yankees, as well as Charlie Keller in the outfield and Tommy Henrich. I remember Joe Gordon at second base and Phil Rizzuto as shortstop. They were great players at a great moment in baseball history. As soon as I reached my sixteenth birthday I could work after 6 p.m. Having made my mark selling peanuts, soda and ice cream at ball games, I applied for a job as a delivery boy at Bergdorf Goodman, the finest department store in New York, located on Fifth Avenue at 58th Street. It was an exciting period of my life because I got to go inside all the posh hotels in Manhattan, where I met many, many celebrities as I delivered their packages. It was really something when I knocked on a door, and Marlene Dietrich opened it for me to deliver her hatbox. I remember it to this day, and, by the way, she did not give me a tip.

Leonard Bernstein's remake of Shakespeare's *Romeo and Juliet*, *West Side Story*, was not at all a fantasy about life in the Bronx or Spanish Harlem. There really were violent gangs, and there was exciting, forbidden, teenage love. It has great music, with some of the authentic rhythms and dancing that we Latins live for. I think music and dancing will always be a vibrant part of Puerto Rican and "Nuyorican" culture. And I loved to dance, even though it was frowned upon in my family's Pentecostal faith. I did, however, enjoy Pentecostal music; it was a powerful bond for sharing our beliefs.

We Puerto Ricans in New York, soon to be called "Nuyoricans," weren't Black or white or Taíno. We were ourselves, with our own way of being, our own mixed traditions. As for myself, I also identified with the Jews. A lot of our neighbors and friends were Jewish, and their delis were the best in New York. I love the Jewish sense of humor, of going forward in the world, their "Here I am, take it or leave it!" attitude.

I recall once when my dad brought home a black friend from work and my mother kept calling him *el americano*. In her eyes, what made him different from her was that he was an English-speaking American, not that he was black. It was language and culture, not color, that distinguished us. We began to be called "Spics" in those days, a put-down that's no longer widely used. And, of course, we

Nuyoricans soon became somewhat different from the island's Puerto Ricans as we picked up different ways from our experience on the continent. We were a little pushier and definitely more street-smart, and those on the island often considered us too aggressive. Of course, our English became better than our Spanish, and we started speaking what people called "Spanglish" as we tried to integrate both languages, another thing that didn't endear us to those who spoke Spanish as their main language.

Our family, like most, had a variety of personalities and looks. My sister Aimee was like me in appearance: mixed, with tan-looking skin, black hair and blue eyes. She had great charisma and exhibited uncommon leadership qualities for a girl back then. Ralph, with the dark eyes of my mother and a darker complexion, was a wonderful older brother, first a soldier in the US Army, then a researcher for Texaco; he was more low key than me. Both he and Aimee were college-educated. My other sister, Estelle, was so fair she couldn't wait to disassociate herself from us, the darker Nuyoricans. She wanted to get out into the world, kick up her heels! Like many others who feel the need to distance themselves from family, she later turned back to us for support when she was dying. But those are all other stories, rich as they may be.

Ah, the South Bronx of those days! But I saw it changing in front of my eyes when I was a young boy. Drugs. When heroin hit the streets, teenagers had to work through many very hard times. Some of my best friends fell to drugs. I was lucky to stay clear. My mom would check my arms for needle tracks by casually stroking my arms when I came home, she was so scared of what was going on. I thought she was being affectionate, but she told me years later that she was checking for needle tracks, just to make sure!

An adolescent boy can be a volatile figure. It was a rough time, very rough. A lot of the boys I played with ended up on drugs and in prison. Supreme Court Justice Sonia Sotomayor is a generation younger than me, but she also grew up in the South Bronx of Puerto Rican parents. In her autobiography, she opines that boys had a harder time of it than girls, because they were free to roam the streets. I remember Sonia Sotomayor's mother very well because she worked for many years at the small Prospect Hospital, which was located in what would later become my congressional district and which was owned by Dr. Jack Friedman, a great community leader. That is where I met Sonia for the first time as a child . . . and now I see her sitting as a member of the United States Supreme Court!

I was a teenager, and like all teenagers, I was unsure of my path or how to get along in life. And I was maybe a bit cocky, the result of some saying I "looked like Burt Lancaster," a popular movie star at the time, because of my height, olive skin and blue eyes. I was diffident in manner but with an underlying *chutzpah* . . . what an ego!

My mother kept harping at me, "A man has to work, if he's a man. Or he's a bum!"

She was vigilant in watching out for me. But I couldn't get a good job without an education. I had jobs just stacking merchandise, being a messenger boy, that sort of thing. I'd started studying, but really didn't like it. So, finally I went down the street and tried to volunteer for the Air Force.

The recruiter said, "They're full up at the moment. But we have space in the Army. How about that?"

Compared to what was available at the time, it sounded okay to me. Our country wasn't at war, so I wasn't afraid of getting shot at. I took the papers home for my mother to sign; I was only seventeen and needed her signature. That was it. I was in the Army.

CHAPTER THREE
Called to Service: Military and Public

The Korean War broke out on June 25, 1950. I had just finished boot camp at Fort Dix, New Jersey and I was sent to Fort Monmouth, New Jersey for a year to study to be a radio operator. In September of 1951, I received orders to go to Korea. I was flown out to California and, there, boarded the USNS *Mitchell* for Yokahama, Japan, assigned to the 3rd Infantry Division, 15th Regiment Combat Team. We were aboard ship for two weeks, then for another week from Japan to Korea. I wasn't put in with the 65th Infantry from Puerto Rico because I had been born in New York. The 65th had a reputation as real daredevils and already had a lot of combat wounded and dead. I was surely proud to serve alongside them.

On my nineteenth birthday, January 9, 1952, we arrived in the west coast of the Korean Peninsula to a bitter, bitter cold. I'll never forget it. It was the coldest I'd been in my life, even with heavy parkas, sleeping bags and tents with little pot-bellied stoves. It almost hurt to breathe, it was so cold. The frigid air felt like it was scraping my lungs. My outfit landed on a secure beach in Inchon, Korea on an LST (landing ship tank) boat, and we tramped ashore on the crunchy, icy earth. We were suddenly in the middle of it and ordered to lay a direct phone wire between the forward observer on the line and our artillery units, better known as batteries.

I was by now considered an expert in communications, using the walkie-talkie in "line of sight," meaning it only worked if there were no obstructions between you and the other walkie-talkie. We also had radio for "out of sight" communication, but we had to change frequencies often since the enemy could intercept our messages. Even with those basic alternatives, effective communication was difficult—this was well before satellites, computers and the internet.

I was assigned to the 39th Field Artillery of the Tennessee National Guard, a mobilized National Guard outfit assigned to the 3rd Infantry Division that needed radio men as forward observers on the front line. The 3rd Division also included a Greek, or Hellenic, Battalion fighting under the United Nations' Resolution on Korea. We were to be sent to Kelly Hill, #317, to support the mostly Puerto Rican 65th Infantry. At the Replacement Depot, we were then fully equipped for combat—something that made us all the more anxious, and with good reason. Men were being maimed and killed all around us. So every soldier had the opportunity to meet with his faith leader. The Catholics and Orthodox prayed with a priest, the Jews with a rabbi and I sought out the Protestant chaplain, who gave a little prayer service before we went on to the line. I remember thinking, "God, just get me out of here alive, and I'll go with Aimee to the Bible College in Missouri. I'll become a pastor."

I wrote my older sister Aimee that same night and told her about my vow. She was, and is, a wonderful sister: a leader, my counsel. She's always been my best friend and spiritual confidant, as well. There used to be a saying, "There are no atheists in the foxholes." I found out it was true. I had become very religious.

At Inchon, we weren't just communications guys. That first night on Kelly Hill I was assigned to guard duty at the perimeter, the 2 a.m. to 4 a.m. shift, the very worst watch. It was a full moon. Our battery was made up of 105mm Howitzers and the din and barrage of both sides' cannons were incredible. I'd never heard artillery before in my life and I was totally unfamiliar with explosives and combat. But there I was behind a machine gun and sandbags, surrounded by the most awful booming noise. The earth really trembled. I'd never heard anything like it. The front line was just a thousand feet way! It wasn't like warfare today, when soldiers often can't even identify who their enemy is. We knew exactly who they were, right there on the other side of the line, right in front of us on the

Main Line of Resistance "MLR," the North Koreans and Chinese were on one side of the line, the United Nations' forces on the other side . . . the good guys on one side and the bad guys on the other, just like in the movies. Soon after the North crossed the 38th Parallel and invaded South Korea, the Chinese had come in to support the North Koreans, making them formidable opponents. They were everywhere, and it seemed there were millions of them. Our patrol was scared they'd run right over us. After two or three incidents when the Chinese troops had almost done just that, our MLR seemed to have become stable enough. Even so, we always had to be on the ready to "move out."

I was stationed there from January to July, and then we were rotated to prepare to go home. A tour of duty was nine months in the Korean War. Being rotated didn't mean we would go back to the United States immediately. We were kept close by, in Japan, to be battle-ready in case a surprise surge arose in Korea. I was sent to serve in Japan with the 21st Regiment and ended up serving sixteen months altogether before being sent home. The nickname of the 21st was the "Gimlets"; it had been the first to fight in Korea in a vicious, bruising battle that saw those poorly prepared troops lose many men. The United States was better prepared for combat by the time I arrived, partly because they kept seasoned troops nearby.

The last couple of months I was deployed back to Camp Schimmelpfennig, Japan, where we were in continual training, with lots of maneuvers including climbing up and down ship nets with heavy knapsacks on our backs to little LSTs moving in the sea. Those were anxious times. I almost thought I was going crazy, I was so nervous. We were expecting to be shipped back to Korea at any moment. Fortunately, though, that was it for me. The Army gave me a Battle Star as well as the experience and friends of a lifetime.

I was finally going home. Back to the USA! I'll never forget driving down Broadway and seeing the bright lights of 42nd Street and hearing the music from the dancehalls. What an incredible upper! Man, how I loved to dance! As for my foxhole vow to become a pastor, I thought, "Thanks for getting me home, Lord. See ya later!" Boy was I ready for the world!

* * *

Thanks to the GI Bill, I started school again, first at the City College of New York and later at the RCA Institute to study electronics. I did well. This was the pre-personal computer days, so computers were gigantic, with hundreds of vacuum tubes in cabinets occupying large rooms. It was a clumsy process, still developing, but the beginning of what would be an incredibly important part of modern life.

After finishing my studies, I was inspired to go to my ancestral home, which I hardly knew. I was off to Puerto Rico to see about work there. I applied at Fomento, the government's industrial development agency, at WAPA's television studios and even looked at IBM.

"*No, gracias,*" they each told me. "Go back to New York, where there are jobs. We don't have enough work for those already here."

In my innocent affection for Puerto Rico, I was bewildered by my reception in Puerto Rico. Some people saw me, the Nuyorican, as some sort of different species. Well, that became an important part of my continuing education in life: learning and discerning how people treat each other. As a young man, still idealistic despite Korea, it was a shock for me to go to the island that had played such a nostalgic role in my family and not be accepted as an equal. Outsiders, even relatives, weren't welcome. We Nuyoricans were different, *distintos*, and therefore were distrusted.

Anyway, I couldn't get a job on an island that was always reeling with unemployment, so it was back to New York City. I took some tests and got a good job at IBM, stayed there for five years and then went to Control Data for four years. I did well. Meanwhile, I met Anita Medina Berríos in 1958. She was divorced and a friend of my cousin. Her dad was Mexican, an undocumented immigrant who'd made his own way, a hardworking man. Anita's mother was a Puerto Rican who had been married to Felipe Torres, an important leader in the Bronx. He was the first Puerto Rican in the Bronx to become a state assemblyman. Her half-brother, Frank Torres, was involved in the local Democratic organization, called The Pontiac Club. He became one of my early mentors.

Anita and I got married in 1959. I adopted Anita's lovely girl, Rozzie, and we had our two sons, Robert and Kenneth. They were wonderful as children: bright, energetic and creative. I was a working man, had a growing family, was active in my church and known around and about as a scoutmaster at St. Peter's Church at 140th Street. I was in the right place at the right time to enter politics. And as we know, timing is everything.

A person's life reflects certain critical moments. Sometimes something happens that drastically affects your whole way of thinking and being. Such a moment happened to me on the corner of Fox and Longwood, just across from P.S. 29 in the South Bronx, in April or May of 1960. Standing there chatting with some people, I encountered Felipe Torres, a Democrat leader in the South Bronx at that time and my wife's relative by marriage. Anita's half-brother was his son, Frank Torres, who went on to become a New York Supreme Court Judge.

Felipe and I talked for some time about Puerto Ricans, civil rights and politics. He saw my eagerness to be involved and gave me some green-lined paper for me to go door to door to get people to sign petitions backing delegates supporting Massachusetts Senator John Fitzgerald Kennedy as the party's presidential nominee at the Democratic National Convention in Los Angeles in July. Each assembly district was made up of election districts, and the district captain was responsible for each person in his district. It was an effective cell structure, dating back to the old Tammany Hall, the infamous, controlling, democratic machine. Even though Felipe had become an assemblyman, he was still also a district captain. He had to not only get the votes out, but had to really know and help his constituents and to get signatures. He needed helpers like me.

The South Bronx in those days didn't have many high-rise buildings. Tenements lined the streets: four-and-five-story apartment buildings and no elevators, of course! I had a list of registered Democratic voters and was supposed to go door to door, knock and explain my mission, get the signature and keep on going. Up and down and up and down I'd go, starting at the bottom, working my way up to the top. Once at the top, I'd go on up to the rooftop, an interesting sort of place used equally for family portraits and for junkies to shoot up. What a strange mix. Often enough, a junkie was shooting heroin directly into his veins. He'd stare up at me with glassy eyes, and I'd say, "Pardon me, fella, I'm just on my way." I'd jump over to the next rooftop and work my way down. Back and forth, building by building.

I came back with fifty or sixty signatures the very first time out and had amassed an impressive amount of signatures by the end of the exercise. It's still clear in my mind as my first real introduction to politics. I was captivated. I liked the give and take of trying to get people together. I was really excited about getting Puerto Ricans to be an integral part of the new civil rights movement. I joined the Torres campaign staff for reform. I was hooked!

John Fitzgerald Kennedy got the Democratic nomination, of course, and narrowly won the White House. Besides being handsome and eloquent, he was a tremendously charismatic leader, especially for the Hispanics and Blacks. He galvanized us and made us want to enter public life. One example of JFK's brilliant use of symbolism was his inviting Governor Luis Muñoz Marín and his wife to the White House for what became an iconic concert by the world-famed cellist Pablo Casals in 1961. Kennedy's invitation of Casals and Governor Muñoz had not only honored Puerto Rico, but Latin America as well, just as he had launched his Alliance for Progress initiative in the hemisphere. Two years later, JFK awarded Muñoz the Presidential Medal of Freedom, the first Puerto Rican to be so honored.

It was also in 1961 that Mayor Robert F. Wagner could not get the endorsement for reelection from the Bronx Regular Democratic machine led by Charles Buckley, who was also a powerful congressman from New York and chairman of the House Committee on Public Works. Wagner then decided to leave the Regular Democratic Organization, defy the bosses and become a Democratic reformer. Felipe Torres had wanted to become a judge, but the Regulars would not support him, and he also split with them. He and his son Frank broke with the Regular Democratic Organization in solidarity with the mayor and became part of the Reform Democratic Organization.

Soon afterward, I went along with Felipe and a group of supporters to meet with Mayor Wagner at City Hall, both to give him
our own endorsement and to seek his permission to name our new
political club in the Bronx after him. It didn't hurt that Mayor Wagner won his reelection bid in 1961 and we were right there with him
on that day. That did it! I was all caught up by then and bitten by the
political bug.

Frank and Felipe Torres founded the Robert F. Wagner Reform
Democratic Club on Prospect and Westchester Ave. Of course, they
were family, and I went right along and became a Reformer with
them. Apparently because of all this enthusiastic work, I received a
surprise call from a wealthy builder in Manhattan by the name of
Jim Scheuer, who was planning a run for Congress from the South
Bronx Congressional District in 1962, which included a good part of
Felipe's assembly district around 138th Street. That was right where
I grew up. He wanted to enlist me on his election team. I accepted,
with the added understanding that I could also work with Frank
Torres, who was running for his father's assembly seat, because
Felipe was retiring to finally fulfill his life's ambition of becoming
a judge. It was a good move for him, and he eventually became a
Family Court Judge in the Bronx.

Jim was running against Congressman Jim Healey, a four-term
incumbent from the West Bronx, in the Democratic primary election
in September which, in the Bronx, is tantamount to a November victory in the general election. Scheuer lost by 2,000 votes, despite our
carrying all the areas I worked, the twelve election districts I was
responsible for.

As it worked out, Frank Torres won his primary by fifty-two
votes over Eugene Rodríguez, an attorney from the Regular Democratic Organization, and went on to win his assembly district by a
wide margin in the general election, once again because Bronx
County is overwhelmingly Democratic, and a victory in the Democratic primary also assured victory in November's general election.

It was a heady victory for the new Reformers. We were the only
reform club that won in the whole county in the 1962 primary for

Congress, and because of it we really got everyone's attention. Now I was really hooked!

Although Jim Scheuer didn't win a seat in Congress that time around, he ran again in 1964, and again he called on me to play a key role in his campaign. That time, he won. But Frank Torres lost his assembly district. Jim held his seat in Congress until the US Census-mandated reapportionment of 1972 that split the district, forcing him to run against incumbent and Regular Democratic Organization Congressman Jack Gilbert . . . and then he won again.

Our South Bronx would deeply mourn the assassination of President Kennedy in November 1963. It shook the whole nation. In the months following JFK's death, President Lyndon B. Johnson led Kennedy's civil rights legislation through Congress. This was not just a political movement, of course, but a movement toward freedom for a whole people. The Civil Rights Act of 1964 banned discrimination based on "race, color, religion or national origin in employment and public accommodations." The Voting Rights Act of 1965 restored and protected voting rights that had been lost since the Reconstruction years following the Civil War. Puerto Rico's US citizens on the island never could, and still can't, vote for president, but back then, many Puerto Ricans on the continent had been denied access to the vote because of poor formal education and lack of literacy in English. A so-called literacy test for English had to be passed in order to get a voter registration card. Our people knew their community and usually could read and write Spanish, but some couldn't read English well. While surrounded by Spanish-speakers, they got along fine without it, just as many other groups had in their own neighborhood enclaves. Because of these civil rights laws, all of that changed and empowered people to vote in their own language.

By this time, Puerto Ricans had basically taken over the famous Pontiac Club from the old establishment. The ethnic winds in the South Bronx were changing, and they were blowing Nuyorican. I'd go over to the club after Boy Scout meetings at St. Peter's, still dressed in my scoutmaster's uniform. The camaraderie was strong, and it was very encouraging just to be there. Ever since that day at

Fox and Longwood with Felipe Torres, and then going to visit voters asking them to sign JFK's nominating petition, nothing would be the same for me. By now I was president of the Adlai Stevenson Democratic Club located on 188th Street in the Bronx. I had a great team with me, and they really were "the wind beneath my wings." Many of them had experience from a number of local elections for everything from school district to county chair, as well as legislative and city council seats in New York. As the saying goes, they had "paid their dues." Together we won some and lost a few . . . but they were loyal to the club, and I loved them all.

George Mora was my brother-in-law, married to my wife Anita's half-sister, Aida. Aida was Frank Torres' sister and Felipe's daughter. George was my most loyal follower, very effective and able in reading election districts and strategizing the right political moves. Joe Noriega, whom I met when he was working for one of my opponents, became my most avid and energetic campaigner. Dorothy Hasbrouck was from the Millwood Housing projects and a leader in the black community. A great lady and wise Latina, Evelina Antonetty, was like our godmother, and we all listened to her wisdom. She was my mentor and a person I came to rely on heavily, a woman devoted to the children of the South Bronx. She worked selflessly without reward and always with just one purpose in mind: to improve the life of the young people, especially students. She made a difference in the lives of many of us, and I will always hold her dear to my heart. She was a true warrior for the poor.

I truly loved the action, loved helping aspiring candidates from our community get elected. At that point, I had never had any thought of putting myself forward as a candidate for public office. I would learn that life often takes a surprising turn, and what happened next certainly surprised me! One of our community activists by the name of Salvador Almeida expressed great interest in running for Frank Torres's assembly seat. He arranged for a meeting to ask for my club's support. I told him I would gladly get my members together as soon as possible to vote on it. I was so sure they would approve that I kind of jumped the gun, when he went on to say that he also wanted me to be his campaign manager. Caught off guard, I hastily said yes.

About a week later, when I finally got my group together at the club and presented Salvador's request to them, they really gave me hell. Everyone was shouting at once, and I had to yell the loudest just to get them quiet. Then they told me, point blank, that if they were going to support anybody for Frank's seat, it would be me. I was stunned! I didn't know what to say, how to react or even what to think, but I did know that this was an important moment for the club's future. If I didn't react, I would lose control of it altogether. I told them that first I would have to go tell Sal Almeida what they had decided. I went to his travel agency office and gave him the bad news. He was not only very disappointed, he was also angry at me for letting him down. It was one tough moment, and I tried to tell him it wasn't personal, but he "let me have it" anyway. But all's well that ends well, and he ran in an adjoining district and won.

With this rocky start, I was launched into the fray, and my club was right there in the thick of it supporting me all the way. I loved them all and worked hard to deserve their support.

Meanwhile, a new world was dawning as a result of the Voting Rights Act. It was an exciting and invigorating time, a great challenge for the young. Martin Luther King Jr. was in DC raising the hopes of black America and those of all races who wanted equality in American society. Marches, picketing and demonstrations were happening all over the United States as people, especially the young, became more aware of the need for reform and a radical re-adjustment of our openly racist society. The Puerto Ricans in our neighborhood were part of that dynamic time. It caused an incredible change in our minority mindset, almost a revolution. It still makes my heart pound to think of those days.

Thank God, for our nation's sake, that Martin Luther King Jr. was a sincere pacifist in his philosophy, because his leadership and his gift of oratory were just riveting and could have been used instead to unleash real street violence. He adopted the non-violent tactics that had helped Ghandi win India its independence from Great Britain. King's leadership helped turn the United States around, ushering Hispanics and women—not just the African Americans—into the mainstream. I can't tell you how strong my passions were and continue to be today for the radical changes King's leadership inspired. While I never had the honor of meeting him, I did get to work on many projects with his widow Coretta Scott King in Atlanta following his assassination in 1968, including the national holiday that honors him each year.

Puerto Ricans, Mexicans, women and African Americans, we all struggled for a place at the table as those new laws, and the politics they created, opened the doors to those on all rungs of society's ladder. President Johnson proved to be a strong defender of, and leader for, the cause. That surprised many, because as a Texan, he'd been associated with the conservative southern Democrats. With the enactment of the Civil Rights Act in 1964 and the Voting Rights Act in 1965 and the programs of LBJ's "Great Society" with its War on Poverty, we suddenly, and for the first time, had the potential of major political and economic clout. Of course, the various minority groups often became rivals for turf and political power; that's just the way of the world. But at last the landless, voiceless people with poor education could finally vote and even seek office! We were all moving forward on the path, sometimes jostling against each other and throwing an occasional elbow to get to the front of the line. But we were going to get there together.

The year 1965 was incredible. I loved being involved in community action, and the timing was perfect. In 1965 a good number of minorities were elected for the first time. I would be among them.

Of the Hispanics elected in New York State, I would last the longest, from 1965 to 1990. As I stated earlier, the Voting Rights Act, the work of Martin Luther King Jr. and President Lyndon B. Johnson had far-reaching implications that changed politics in America forever and affected the make-up of legislatures around the country, in many cases improving access for minority groups. Based on the census figures of the decade, districts are re-drawn by each state legislature. Voting patterns may change accordingly each decade, depending on many factors. After the Voting Rights Act, districts needed to reflect new realities. To comply with the act, special elections were being held to open the doors to minorities so they could be fairly represented and their districts not get "gerrymandered," that is cut and scattered to other legislative districts. It mandated that congressional districts had to be "compact and contiguous," but still with the same number of people in each district, thereby removing with the stroke of a pen the "at-large legislative seats." Prior to this, members of Congress often had districts covering many miles in areas that were unrelated and not contiguous. Because of the Voting Rights Act, minorities could now choose and elect someone like themselves from their own neighborhoods and minorities could begin to climb the political ladder to parity. If the communities were not satisfied with the configuration of their districts, they could go to the US Department of Justice and make the case that, in fact, their minority group in question had been cut out of a particular district.

Many at the time believed it was a boon just for Blacks, but I was certainly one of the first Hispanics to benefit. In New York, the elections for legislative offices are held every two years, and the 1965 election would be for a special one-year term only, to be followed by another election the following year. If I won, no sooner had I gotten into public office, then I'd had to start thinking immediately about running for reelection. The Constitution of New York states clearly there should be 150 Assembly seats. (The NY Senate doesn't have the same requirement.) In 1965, to comply with the Voting Rights Act, the Assembly momentarily jumped to 165 seats, just to give entry to the new districts created after the census. In 1966 there would be another election, and it would go back to the constitutionally required 150 seats, meaning 15 positions would be eliminated. That would mean a lot of scrambling in this new game of "musical chairs."

Puerto Rican Herman Badillo, a sharp, hard working, self-made man, had already shot up through Democratic party ranks and was much involved in East Harlem politics. He'd successfully organized the Kennedy for President Committee there. Then he moved to the Bronx, where he was elected borough president in 1965. Badillo was vigorously backed by the leading Hispanic newspaper of the day, *El*

Diario-La Prensa, owned by O. Roy Chalk, also owner of Trans Caribbean Airlines, the largest airline operating between San Juan and New York City. Governor Muñoz Marín, leader of the Popular Democratic Party (PDP) in Puerto Rico, allied with mainland Democrats and helped back the slate that Badillo had worked out for the Democratic primaries. Badillo would be leading the slate as the candidate for Bronx borough president. He had a lot of momentum going for him.

As it happened, he did win, though barely. Badillo later became the first island-born congressman although, I was happy and proud to win fairly comfortably. Three other Puerto Ricans also won, helped significantly by our Popular Democratic Party friends from the island. The Puerto Rico Migrant Office strongly encouraged people to vote and to find representation in government. It made a vast difference in the turnout and our success.

Four Puerto Rican assemblymen, including me, were elected. I doubt very much if I would have been elected that first time if Badillo had not been on the slate. I was off to Albany and a new career!

In 1966, I also became the first and, for a while, the only Puerto Rican charter member of the newly formed New York Assembly Black/Puerto Rican Caucus. We were four Puerto Ricans in the assembly: Gil Ramírez (Brooklyn), Salvador Almeida (Bronx), José Ramos López (East Harlem and Manhattan) and me. The other three refused to join the Blacks in a caucus; I was the only one to step up, allowing it to be known as the Black and Puerto Rican Caucus! Later on, the others did join; the rivalry between the Blacks and Puerto Ricans had calmed down with the years, as we all learned how to handle a new access to power that we'd never had before.

From 1967 to 1978, the voters continued to elect me to the New York Senate, with my Democratic colleagues choosing me as deputy minority leader in 1975. In 1976 the party chose me as a delegate to the Democratic National Convention—my star was rising!

CHAPTER FOUR

Winning my Stripes in New York Politics

When I made the decision to run for public office in 1965, never did I dream that I would be a pioneer in a profession that was so all-encompassing. You get elected from an assembly district within your state, always assuming that representing your constituents is your primary responsibility and you'll be doing nothing else. But you soon learn the art of trading with your colleagues, so that your district can get the necessary votes for projects that you seek for your own community.

The very first things I learned as a state assemblyman were the importance of your keeping your word and the need to get along with your colleagues . . . regardless of party. Relationships were extremely important; I had to be a good listener and have patience, always remembering that we assemblymen are merely caretakers and that it's not about us; it's about the people we represent. As an assemblyman from the South Bronx I had to start voting on projects dealing with places as far away as Buffalo, Plattsburgh, Syracuse, Yonkers . . . right to the northern tip of Long Island. These were areas I was also responsible for. As a state legislator, my jurisdiction was the entire State of New York and everything within its boundaries.

From 1967 to 1975 I was the first and only Hispanic in the Senate of New York. In 1975 Israel Ruiz, also from the Bronx, joined me. The State Senate was a great proving ground that prepared me for the United States Congress, and I truly enjoyed the twelve years

I spent there. The last three years, when I was selected as minority leader of the Senate, were very special because right before the 1970 elections, districts were reapportioned again to create a minority seat in the South Bronx. For the first time, a congressional district representing the South Bronx was created to comply with the Voting Rights Act of 1965. The New York Assembly redrew the state, and the resulting district was solidly Puerto Rican, with some Blacks. Herman Badillo, who had previously been elected Bronx borough president, won that seat handily in 1970 and was in Congress from 1971 until 1977, when he became the deputy mayor of New York under Ed Koch. The reapportionment also forced Jim Scheuer to run against Jack Bingham, the powerful incumbent from the North Bronx, and Jim lost.

By nature, I'm a listener, oftentimes a mediator. Now that I'm older, the listening part increases. In those days of hot, active youth, rushing ahead to meet life, I spoke up far more. I was starting to learn to roar. But I was still learning. When standing up to speak the first time, I didn't really know what I was doing! Being a novice in the specialized world of the Assembly was quite an experience . . . even more so being Puerto Rican in a sub-group of Democrats in a Republican-dominated legislature.

How does one learn? By experiencing the give and take, the listening and the talking. But listening is most important of all. Since I was a boy meandering around New York City, learning the lay of the land, I'd listen to everyone. All that time I never realized what a great preparation it would someday be for entering politics. I love to talk to people, to listen to their stories and engage in conversation, regardless of a person's age, color, dress or gender. You need to really listen, not just hear. That's in my blood.

Of course, I'm from a working-class family, and my father was a union man through and through. We Democrats have always been tight with the unions for obvious reasons and committed to labor rights. One of the major unions represented in the South Bronx is the New York Transport Workers Union (TWU), which was among my first constituents. Some TWU leaders visited me in Albany to ask me to present a bill. In the legislative process, huge numbers of bills are presented, many without the slightest possibility of passing. But the very fact that a bill is presented demonstrates action. And that's important. One of the TWU leaders who had come up was a Puerto Rican named Dámaso Seda, a good guy, and I was happy to help out to the best of my modest ability. I got the bill presented and they were pleased.

The very next year, the TWU representatives showed up again and asked me to reintroduce the same bill.

"Where's Dámaso?" I asked.

"Our budget's been cut, so he couldn't come," they said.

"Well, I can't do anything about this unless he's here with you. I consider him a key player jumping from unions to prisons."

By now I realized the power of the office and that I could help build up my fellow Puerto Rican, in this case so Dámaso would be considered important in the union's leadership. They left. They returned with the bill and Dámaso in hand. I presented it. Some years later, Dámaso was elected president of the union. I was proud of him and that perhaps I'd played a small part in helping him move forward.

Meanwhile, with President Johnson not seeking reelection in 1968 due to the war in Vietnam, I endorsed civil rights advocate and New York Senator Bobby Kennedy over New Hampshire's Senator Eugene McCarthy. I had planned an event for Kennedy in Manhattan for June 8, a few days after the California Democratic primary, which he won. After watching his victory speech in the Ambassador Hotel ballroom the night of the primary, I went to bed feeling that his campaign had just gained unstoppable momentum. At three or four in the morning, my phone rang; it was my sister Aimee.

"Have you heard the news?" she asked.

I mistook her anxiety for excitement and answered, "It's great! Bobby's gonna go all the way!"

"He's been shot, Bobby."

I don't remember the next thirty seconds at all, but Aimee later told me that I had been stunned into silence.

Our event was naturally canceled, but I was pleased that Puerto Ricans were chosen among the officials asked to serve as honorary pall bearers in the memorial service at St. Patrick's Cathedral. Our contingent included high-ranking people from the island, including Luis Negrón López and Victor Pons and, from New York, José Monserrat—all members of the island's Popular Democratic Party—and me. The next day, we were all shuttled down to DC by train for his burial next to his brother, JFK, in the National Cemetery in Arlington. It was an honor and a moving experience; one I remember as though it were yesterday.

With the bitter feelings about the continuing deaths in the Vietnam War and the rising conflict as various groups approached the shifting civil rights movement with different motives and factions, Republican Richard Nixon was elected president and Nelson Rockefeller was elected governor of New York.

Prison Reform

It was in the late 1960s as I served in the New York Senate that I became a staunch advocate of prison reform and prisoner rehabilitation; along the way I had also become the ranking member of the Senate's Crime and Corrections Committee. Many of my fellow Puerto Ricans were being sent to prison for drugs, and I had to know what was happening.

Christ had said, "I was in prison, and did you visit me?"

On a purely personal level, I answered that question by visiting prisoners with my sister Aimee, who by now had followed our father and was a pastor in her own right. For her part, she was becoming very well known among Evangelical Christians (statewide and even around the nation) as an inspired preacher. I've said it before here and I'll say it again: My sister has always been my beloved mentor. Even now as she grows older and frail, she maintains her charisma. "Acorns do not fall too far from the tree"; her daughter Debbie and son Joseph have become exceptional ministers as well and gifted in music, something they inherited from their talented musician father, Joseph Cortese. In 1986, her daughter Damaris won an OTI Award (an international Spanish-language song festival) as "Best Singer" and has made her mark singing Christian music. I am so blessed to have all of them, and their spouses, as family.

But back to New York's prisons in the late 1960s. On official visits, the Republican Crime and Corrections Committee chairman John Dunne and Nassau County Senator Ralph Marino (Ralph became a good friend) and I, as the ranking Democrat, would go to prisons throughout the state and New York City to talk to inmates about conditions in the prison. In the various facilities we visited, the warden would usually select those he wanted us to speak with. Then I would insist on choosing others from the rank and file at random—two whites, two Blacks, two Hispanics—to see how they were being treated and what opportunities for rehabilitation they were being offered. On one of those visits, a South Bronx Puerto Rican, Roy Calderón, really impressed me. He was serving time for burglarizing the empty homes of the wealthy but seemed to have a good spirit. I thought that, given the chance, he would not return to a life of crime. I promised him a job when he got out, and he ended up working for me as a caseworker for about ten years. After that, he went back to the Department of Corrections, but this time to work, and when he died the department gave him a tremendous send-off: full honors and a white-glove burial. Roy was a good person . . . and a living testament to the possibilities of rehabilitation.

At any rate, I was building up a good reputation with the inmates and joined various associations for prison reform. By the early seventiess, the tremendous racial tensions were reflected in the nation's prisons. There were so many Blacks in prison, a much higher percentage than their numbers in the general population. More Hispanics, too. Overall conditions were as bad as they usually are in prison. Violent criminals were housed next to non-violent offenders. Sexual attacks on the young and weaker were almost a given. There were no opportunities for rehabilitation, no Spanish-speaking staff and no possibilities for Muslim worship services. That was during the time that the black Muslims were in the news and growing in the United States under the leadership of Elijah Muhammad, Malcolm X and Muhammad Ali. There was overt, institutionalized racism in our prisons as both Blacks and Hispanics were particularly mistreated.

Often called to negotiate with or on behalf of prisoners, I found myself in such a role at the largest prison riot in US history in September 1971: Attica. The full story follows, but the lasting and horrifying duty of counting the dead bodies stretched out on the prison's concrete yard impressed upon me the importance of continuing dialogue . . . no matter what. There is always time to die.

There's a relevant saying in Spanish: *En las guerras anunciadas, no hay muertos* (In pre-announced wars, there are no deaths).

The Attica Prison Riot

The largest and most violent prison riot in US history began on September 9, 1971 at the Attica State Prison in upstate New York. More than 1,000 prisoners had taken control of Prison Yard D and held several dozen prison employees as hostages. Many of the prisoners were Black or Puerto Rican, and the guards were all white non-Hispanics. Because of my experience in prison reform and being a New York State senator of Puerto Rican heritage, I was asked to join the observer commission for negotiations that Governor Nelson Rockefeller named to help in the arbitration process.

Puerto Rican Herman Badillo, then a US congressman, was our arbitration group's leader. A state plane picked us up at La Guardia Airport and flew us to Wyoming County, where Attica was located. I'd been there before to check out conditions. When we landed, it was the usual grey, cool, misty fall day of upstate New York. We got off the plane not knowing what to expect and were immediately driven to the prison. It looked like some kind of weird castle in the gloom, guard turrets and all. The warden received us at the gate, told us about the situation, then took us to the yard.

During the initial days of the riot, the warden acceded to twenty-eight of the inmate's thirty-one demands, such as food and sanitary conditions, rehabilitation possibilities and so on, most of which were in fact on the books already. The laws simply had not been followed. However, one unmovable obstacle to the rioters' demand for amnesty was the fact that on Thursday, the riot's first day, they had

severely wounded a guard. By Saturday morning he was dead, and
the district attorney said the felony-murder rule applied: they were
all guilty. No blanket amnesty was possible by law.

We walked into a sweaty, rough, uneasy crowd, hundreds of
inmates milling around. I'd been in enough prisons to be saddened,
though not really frightened at that point, by the scene in the yard.
Then I heard voices shouting, "Bobby! Bobby Garcia!"

My Lord, it was guys from the old neighborhood! I looked for
the source and gave a little wave to acknowledge them. The head
inmates, many with towels covering their faces, were sitting at tables
with microphones set up. Forty-two prison guards and workers who
had been taken as hostages were sitting in the middle of the yard. As
usual, the Hispanics were hanging together somewhere in the middle
of the crowd, dominated by the more aggressive Blacks. And of
course, much of the problem was the tribal racial situation as much
as anything.

Herman Badillo spoke first, clearly, with obvious sincerity about
the need for mediation. Badillo was followed by ACLU board member and lawyer, William Kunstler and Tom Wicker from *The New
York Times*. I think he'd already written articles criticizing prison
conditions. I was supposed to speak after Wicker when someone
shouted, "They're coming in!" apparently referring to the state
troopers that Governor Rockefeller had threatened to call up to
retake the prison.

An inmate grabbed the microphone away from Wicker, and
other prisoners doused the lights. The inmate's press conference was
over. The tension . . . the fear . . . were real. Before I knew it, about
ten or eleven Puerto Rican prisoners came and made a circle around
me in the dark, saying, "Nothing's going to happen to you, Bobby.
We've got your back. We're here—*Estamos aquí*."

Within the chaos, a strange feeling of calm came over me. I'll
never forget that moment. And nothing did happen. It had been a
false alarm.

After we were led out of the prison by the inmates, we found a
hotel and spent the next couple of days—it seemed like forever—
going into the prison to negotiate. During those meetings, Black

Panther leader Bobby Seale would talk and, instead of diffusing the situation, his words inflamed the situation, making things much more difficult for negotiations between us and the prisoners. Senate Corrections Committee Chairman John Dunne decided we should call Governor Rockefeller and ask him to come to Attica. Congressman Badillo talked to Rockefeller. Several of those involved kept referring to the Bible and saying, "There's always time to die . . . let's keep talking."

I called my sister Aimee and asked her to pray for us. It was such a hard, tense situation, one that seemed to have no end; the negotiations were going nowhere. The prison guards, on edge with their fellow workers taken hostage, assumed we were totally sympathetic to the inmates. And when they brought us negotiators food, one guard said to me, "I didn't know it was for you. I wouldn't have brought it!"

On Monday morning, September 12, 1971, Governor Rockefeller actually called in the New York State Police troopers. As usual, it was a grey overcast day, and some of us were already inside. Prison officials locked us in a room, but we could hear helicopters clacking and a loudspeaker blaring, "Lay down your arms!" Teargas canisters quickly came through the already broken windows and filtered throughout the buildings. We had no masks, so we pulled our shirts up over our heads to breathe. The troopers, accompanied by local police, came in shooting, and Badillo was heard murmuring, "It's going to be a massacre."

Twenty-nine inmates and ten hostages were killed. Eighty-nine more were wounded. Even after my having served in Korea, it was a horrible sight, all those bullet-riddled dead men lined up on a platform for all of us to see, to witness. I will never in my life forget it. We left Attica . . . shaken and saddened.

Later, autopsies showed they were all—prisoners and hostages—killed by law enforcement bullets, not by having their throats slit as it had been first reported in the media. After the riot, torture and beatings occurred as the guards punished the prisoners for the riot. And years later, the courts found the New York State government at fault and awarded $12 million to the families of the dead.

My take? Conditions inside should never have been allowed to deteriorate so, and I'd said so on previous visits. But no one paid attention to me. I wasn't the decision-maker. That experience impacted me so much (How could it not?) that prisoner rehabilitation became a major issue for me, and I became more active in prison ministry on a personal basis. I argued for prison reform in the legislature. It was an uphill battle. Most officials and their constituents didn't even want to think about it.

Looking back at the transcripts of the McKay Commission hearings—named for the dean of the NYU Law School—and reading media reports, I saw a confusing mishmash. Twenty-nine convicts and ten hostages were killed and another eighty-nine were wounded. During the riots three prisoners were murdered by fellow prisoners or guards. Those responsible were never found. Rockefeller was criticized for not having visited the prison personally to intervene and for having too quickly resorted to lethal force to subdue the inmates.

I'm no expert on that very deep subject. But I have learned that we must awake as a nation to the importance of community volunteer associations to work in prison ministry, and the government needs to have serious rehabilitation programs for prisoners and aid to prisoners' families and children. This is a forgotten part of our America today.

Soon after Attica, I got a call from Mayor John Lindsay, asking me to go to Long Island to mediate in another prison standoff. I remember my son Robert saying, "Daddy, don't go!" Obviously, the coverage of the Attica riot had terrified him. I went to the prison with politician Shirley Chisholm and Nation of Islam leader Louis Farrakhan. We talked with a turbaned guy holding a knife to a guard's throat. We realized all too well how the guard could get killed and how it could explode into something involving dozens.

Farrakhan, known more for his bombastic speaking style, showed a different side of his personality. He was *smooooth*. He was *gooood*. "Brother, let him go," he said quietly and firmly.

The inmate hesitated, then put his knife down, and that particular situation was resolved, thank God.

In searching for better answers to prison conditions and realizing how badly prisoners needed spiritual advisors, I began a close alliance with Reverend Mark Strong, an official with the Assemblies of God Church in Missouri. For the first time in the history of the New York State Department of Corrections, we were able to bring bilingual ministers into prisons as chaplains and have working-class volunteers become part of the effort as well. At this same time, my sister was named as the first woman chaplain in the New York State prison system, assigned to Bedford Hills Women's Corrections Facility.

Punitive Drug Laws and Prison Overpopulation

In 1973, two years after Attica, Governor Rockefeller led the passing of laws requiring judges to impose mandatory sentences of fifteen years-to-life imprisonment for anyone convicted of selling two ounces, or possessing four ounces, of narcotic drugs. New York's prison population soared, and that law accounted for 45% of New York's new prisoners between 1987 and 1997. Other states followed suit, and America's prison population soared fivefold between 1980 and 2009. During that time, in the South Bronx and Harlem, a quarter of the children saw a parent imprisoned. Yet in the South Bronx only 3% of the convictions were for non-drug use felonies.

In 2011, *The Economist* condemned the "draconian sentencing laws that now unnecessarily keep huge numbers of entirely non-violent inmates behind bars: for smoking dope or writing bad checks, say, or for missing parole appointments."

In May 2011, the US Supreme Court ordered California to make prisons more humane. The court found the state guilty of "cruel and unusual treatment" and conditions "incompatible with the concept of human dignity." Overcrowding was rampant, with prisons about 175% full. In the hearings leading up to the decision, Judge Sonia Sotomayor agreed that overcrowding leads to more violence, desperately poor health and mental care and more deaths and suicides. Calling it as it is, she said for the court record, "When are you going to avoid, or get around, people sitting in their feces for days in a dazed state?"

Just how we should approach the plague of drugs is still unclear. Nothing seems to work. People such as Federal Appellate Court Judge Juan Torruella have spoken clearly against the criminalization of drug use, calling it a useless and expensive way to approach a nationwide problem that should be treated as a public health issue, emphasizing treatment and harm-reduction.

Welfare Education

As a state senator I remember the day that Carolyn Maloney and John Ahearn showed up at my office in Albany and asked if I would assist them in getting a grant for a program called "Welfare Education," a program designed to educate folks who were on welfare. Carol Maloney was then an instructor with the program. Both Maloney and Ahearn worked for a solid two-to-three months in Albany, following my suggestion and visiting the senators who had jurisdiction over the funding that could keep the Welfare Education Program going. But it wasn't easy. The Assembly was controlled by the Republicans, the Senate was controlled by the Republicans and the governor was Republican Nelson Rockefeller. The last week of the session a bill appeared on the desks of each senator calling for a $2 million appropriation for extension of the Welfare Education Program. I scanned the senators and my eyes rested on a senator from Syracuse by the name of John Hughes, who had the title of "Mr. Conservative." He was outraged when he saw this legislation on his desk and immediately demanded to know where it had come from and who had submitted it.

With some twenty-five years of service—from 1947 until his death in 1972—Hughes was one of the most powerful men in the state Senate and respected by every Republican. I knew at that moment that we were in real trouble because he could stop the bill's consideration immediately; I felt certain he would try. I realized that I needed to do something and was fortunate that the Republicans' Nassau County chairman, Joseph Margiotta, was a sitting assemblyman and, more importantly, I knew that there were six Republican state senators from Nassau County.

Without saying a word to anyone, I walked over to the Assembly and just began chatting with Margiotta on the outside chance he would give me a hand and have the six Republican senators from Nassau County support this legislation. I knew if I could get those six votes, we could pass this program.

At that very moment, he was in the middle of a debate on the floor of the Assembly but asked me to hold on, that as soon as he finished, he would join me in the Senate and talk to Nassau County senators. True to his word, he did, and the bill passed. I, along with Maloney and Ahearn, owed it all to Joe Margiotta and his six Nassau County Republicans.

In today's political climate, that would not be possible. That was a time when the leaders in political parties talked to each other . . . more interested in doing what was right for the people than always being right themselves.

Another example occurred in 1974, when Boricua College was founded, primarily for Puerto Rican and Hispanic students in the City of New York. Its founder was Víctor Alicea, who remains to this day president of the college. As a state senator I was called upon by both Alicea and Augie Rivera to see if I could help them obtain funding from the state legislature. I was able to secure approximately four hundred thousand dollars for the school. Today Boricua College has campuses in three boroughs of the City of New York; it has made a huge difference in the lives of many young Puerto Ricans and Latinos in the area. I was later honored to be asked to serve on the board of the college.

Nuyorican and Puerto Rican Politics

The 1970s were perilous times. It was a decade of discovery and of change bordering on chaos, it seemed to us. Media pictures of South Bronx streets back then showed burning cars, graffiti-covered walls, mounted police on horseback brandishing nightsticks, grime, drugs and dirt. It was very, very hard to know how to act with good judgment and foresight. It was a real challenge for me to just keep my balance and be effective.

As a state senator I worked intensively with colleagues serving the Nuyoricans. One of those was Joe Monserrat, who had run the Puerto Rico Migrant Division of the Puerto Rico Department of Labor in New York City from 1951 to 1969. He was a great worker and a great guy; originally, he had been appointed by Governor Muñoz Marín. His office provided major help in finding jobs and housing for the migrants and also monitored the wages and treatment of the seasonal agricultural workers who came up from the island to work the fields. The division even issued ID cards documenting that Puerto Rican workers were US citizens, because if they spoke no English, they could be assumed to be undocumented. Now, they could easily have gotten US passports, since they were citizens, but why should they, if they only need to move from one US territory to another? For good reason, that was not the political path chosen, plus it would have cost them the considerable fee for a passport.

As I'd mentioned, the *Populares* (National Popular Party) from Puerto Rico made themselves a major influence in Nuyorican politics. For some reason, Republicans and statehooders never tapped into that power base! And that's the way politics should be run: you back your own, but talk to everyone; if the occasion arises, you can work together. One thing is certain, however: the *Populares* helped me and other Democrats and helped the Nuyoricans.

In 1969 the relatively new and pro-statehood New Progressive Party (NPP) shook up island politics by electing its founder, Ponce industrialist Luís A. Ferré, as the island's governor. In those days statehooders were traditionally allied with the Republican Party in mainland politics. Ferré was known as Puerto Rico's "Mr. Republican." The NPP would soon expand its influence in mainland politics when a pro-statehooder was elected mayor of San Juan: Carlos Romero Barceló. But he declared himself a Democrat. As far as my Nuyorican community was affected, Governor Ferré was a Republican, and it was no surprise he named Republican Manuel A. Casiano, a self-made Nuyorican businessman from the South Bronx, to run Puerto Rico's New York Migrant Office. Suddenly, that office would no longer be such an exclusively Democratic Party stronghold. Nevertheless, the Nuyoricans of the South Bronx continued to be overwhelming loyal to the Democrats and their *Popular* party friends from the island.

Casiano was very sharp. He had been very successful with his own film effects business operating in New York and Hollywood. He had retired at forty-five, enjoyed flying his own plane and living on Park Avenue. Governor Ferré realized his success was a model of initiative, and he asked Casiano first to head the Migrant Division and then Fomento, Puerto Rico's Economic Development Administration, something that required him to live in Puerto Rico; he accepted both.

Once confirmed by Puerto Rico's Senate, Casiano called me from Fomento and asked me to help amend a bill under consideration: the New York State Assembly's bill to "Buy American." He wanted to make sure the language specifically included Puerto Rico as a way to create jobs on the island. Then, as now, many mainlanders didn't realize that Puerto Ricans are US citizens by birth. We soon developed a good working relationship and remained good friends ever since.

After serving in government, Casiano started the weekly newspaper *Caribbean Business*, which developed into Puerto Rico's and the Caribbean's "business bible," as it became the most successful business publication in the region for the next forty-three years. He went on to become the publisher of another eleven publications and the island's first contact center. Casiano Communications became the largest US Hispanic-owned publisher of magazines and periodicals, and "Manny" was always a loyal supporter of my career.

Breaking into the Big Time

Just a month after the Attica riot, I got a call from Maine Senator Edmund Muskie's staff, who asked me to join George Mitchell on his private jet and attend the National Governors' Conference being held that year in Puerto Rico. Of course, I said yes. It was my first flight in a private jet! George Mitchell, then chairman of Maine's Democratic Party, was emerging as an important power broker at the national level. At the time, Muskie was considered the frontrunner for the Democratic nomination for president, so it couldn't hurt to get closer to his organization. The young man from the South Bronx was starting to keep some very distinguished company.

In retrospect, I was out of my league. I was only thirty-eight and still a state legislator, now hanging not on a corner in the Bronx, but with the "big guys" on the national scene.

I recall Muskie asking me, "What could you have done differently in the Attica uprising? Would anything else have worked?"

I looked at him and kind of shrugged my shoulders. While I had often thought about it, my honest answer was, "I really don't know."

He just turned away.

Looking back, I realize my sense of judgment was still developing. My answer now is: We should have kept on talking, and something positive perhaps would have emerged; we would continue to hope, while still preparing to take action if needed. Perhaps violence would ultimately still have been the outcome, but we would have left the door open longer for a potential peaceful resolution. And Rockefeller should have gone personally to the scene to change the dynamics. Of course, hindsight is 20/20.

It was a well-attended conference in San Juan, and I was glad to participate, reuniting with some of my friends from Puerto Rico and from throughout the Democratic Party. Governor Rockefeller was there and was as cordial as always.

There's a great saying in Spanish, "*Dime con quién andas y te diré quién eres.*" (Similar to the English, "You can tell who a person is by the company he keeps.") It surely applied to Governor Ferré's way of thinking. After saying hello as the conference's host governor, he asked me, "Did you come down with Muskie on Mitchell's jet?" Of course, I replied that I had. I was proud to have been invited. But both were prominent Democrats, and the Governor (Mr. Republican in P.R.) didn't talk to me the rest of the time I was there.

As we know, you back your own in politics, and this was the first time, after many years of battle, that Ferré was in the executive position. This was the first time in his long lifetime the statehooders and, by extension, the Republicans had won in Puerto Rico. Ferré was still feeling a bit partisan, I guess. I must say, though, that was not the way he truly was. Later on, we developed a good working relationship. And I worked with his inspiring sister, nun Sor Isolina, first in New York and then in Ponce, where she energized the poor neighborhood where my mother had grown up: La Playa de Ponce.

Back in New York City, I hosted many a celebrity-heavy fundraiser for the Democratic Party and various charities at the Rainbow Room at the top of 30 Rockefeller Plaza and at the Starlight Roof at the Waldorf-Astoria Hotel. They were the "in" places in those days, and many flew up from Puerto Rico just for those events. What a great feeling to see so many Puerto Ricans from the mainland and the island celebrating together! By that time we'd broken into the nation's theatre world, with great dancers like Rita Moreno and actors like José Ferrer, the first Latino and Puerto Rican to win an Oscar. Of course, our musicians had already entered the top tier: percussionist Tito Puente, classical soprano Graciela Rivera, pianists Jesús María Sanromá and cellist Pablo Casals. We claimed some outstanding athletes, too, such as Roberto Clemente and Cheguí Torres.

Among the celebrities was Herman Badillo, the first native-born Puerto Rican elected to Congress as a voting representative. A self-made man, he was both brilliant and focused. Born in Caguas, south of San Juan, he was eleven when both parents died of tuberculosis, a big killer in those days, especially on the island. His aunt in New York sent for him, and he was shuttled around the family. Badillo put himself through college, law school and CPA accreditation. This, even though in his day New York Hispanics and Blacks were almost automatically put on vocational tracks instead of a college track.

Many minority kids use sports to escape an impoverished upbringing. But Badillo had realized that education and politics were a better way to emerge from poverty and discrimination. He resigned from Congress in 1977 to become deputy mayor of New York under Ed Koch and later left the Koch administration over a policy decision. He had always aspired to be the first Latino mayor of the city, but never made it.

I've always admired him greatly for how he blazed the path for Hispanics. True, he could be amazingly arrogant; he had what my Jewish friends call *chutzpah* (I won't say what my Spanish-speaking friends would call it). He didn't like to give credit to anyone but himself. He really was arrogant. But, boy, did he have something to be proud of! He passed away in 2014, and I can only imagine his spirit exploding when President Obama signed a bill in 2015 renaming a Bronx post office, in the Morrisania neighborhood, in his honor as the first Puerto Rican-born US congressman. That was added to the numerous schools and other institutions named for him during his lifetime.

My Path to Congress

As a lifelong Democratic stalwart, I was elected as a Republican and liberal to the United States Congress and then had to petition the Democratic Caucus to be allowed back into the fold. It's an odd tale, but South Bronx politics can be odd. In fact, Badillo fled the party after leaving Ed Koch's city hall to become a Republican and enter private enterprise. But in the fall of 2011, he became a Democrat again, saying he wanted to focus on Hispanic education, which in fact had always been one of his missions. Anyway, Badillo was a leader in the national Democratic Party and he anointed me to fill his seat as a member of the United States House of Representatives when he decided to run for mayor of New York.

I'd been doing a good job in the New York State Senate and had developed a good reputation. At first, I couldn't decide if I really wanted to run for Congress, since I was so happy in the state senate. I was a big fish in a small pond. I was free to do other work, I had a car and driver, had a lot of freedom to choose my areas of involvement, felt comfortable and was still challenged by my work and by serving my constituents. In Congress I would suddenly be a small fish in a big pond.

I talked it over with another Nuyorican, an upcoming fellow who promised to have a great future, José Serrano. He said he wanted it if I didn't, but that I should be the first one considered by the party, and he encouraged me to go forward. (Years later when I left Congress, José took my place. He's there still and doing a very good job.)

Jimmy Carter was president. My friend Nelson Díaz, a White House Fellow working with Vice President Walter F. Mondale's staff, invited me to Washington and to think seriously about this opportunity. He tried to convince me to run for the position while I did the rounds with him in DC. The possibility of being part of the national scene convinced me, and after mulling it over a great deal, I decided to throw my hat into the ring. Since the South Bronx is more than 90% Democratic, it should have been a "done deal." And because it wasn't a regular election, but a special election to fill Badillo's seat, there wouldn't be any primary in the district.

I also talked to Pat Cunningham, the last Irishman to head the Democratic Party as county leader of the Bronx. He headed up the committee to choose the Democratic candidate for general election; unfortunately, he had his own favorite . . . and it wasn't me. He just would not choose me for the nomination despite Badillo's backing. That really got my competitive juices flowing. I was furious and talked to my friend in the state Senate, John Calandra, who was county leader for the Bronx Republicans.

He said, "If that SOB won't give you the nomination, I'll give you the Republican nomination!"

And so he did. Consequently, I ran on the Republican and liberal line against five other people on different party lines, including an independent.

CHAPTER FIVE

Mr. Garcia Goes to Congress

My district elected me to Congress in the special election on Valentine's Day, 1978. In spite of a heavy snow, a lot of people turned out to vote. I hadn't been sure I could win, having to run on the Republican ticket and spurning Democratic county leader Pat Cunningham's supposed control of my party. I sought my community's backing and knew that surely some of the voters were a bit confused, seeing Bob Garcia, their lifelong Democratic leader, identified on the wrong side.

I got support from several surprising sources. One was from two young rabbis at a synagogue on Pelham Parkway. They took me to meet about 200 ladies at the Daughters of Jacob Home for the Elderly. Most of these women were from Eastern European Jewish stock and had migrated from the lower East Side to the Bronx. By now, many of their children had moved out to the more prosperous suburbs, leaving these tough ladies to "hold the fort" in the Bronx. Traditionally they voted Democrat, since they tended to be union sympathizers and liberal in their philosophy, carried over from President Franklin Delano Roosevelt days. They were stalwarts.

When I was introduced to them, one of them burst out, "Me? I should vote for a Republican? You should break my arm!" She was a really wise gal, with that inimitable *chutzpah* that I appreciate and even emulate when necessary.

I grinned and said, "This is South Bronx politics, ya' know."

I explained the situation, and they caught on fast. I think the whole group voted for me, every single one. Those who were infirm

49

and couldn't enter the narrow voting booths were helped out by the two young rabbis, sometimes staying with them behind the curtain, to make their marks. Obviously, I wasn't with them that day, but that's what I heard.

I remember some other voting day images. I'm walking through my turf, shaking hands with everyone in sight on 138th and Brook, and I came across a wiry Puerto Rican guy, a staunch Democrat from the neighborhood, who held out his hand and said, "Garcia! I voted for you! But you're a Republican? I couldn't believe it!" He almost had tears in his eyes. I explained the Pat Cunningham problem and he calmed down. Then, I remember visiting the commuters at the subway station on 149th and Third, asking for their vote. Carol Bellamy, president of the city council, was with me. In those days, the power of New York City resided in the powerful trio who made up the Board of Estimate: the president of the city council, the comptroller and the mayor. (The City Charter has since changed that structure.) Carol and I had become good friends when I was in the state Senate. Later on, she would head up the Peace Corps, then became ambassador to UNICEF as well as occupying many other important positions. She was a very good person, hardworking and kind. She and many others from the Democratic Party turned out in full force to back me, the Republican.

The South Bronx was about 95% Democratic and had always been. In the old days, they'd close the streets and have bonfires and parties the night before elections to rev up the voters. That no longer happened, but it was no secret that our party was still dominant. This time, though, I was running on the Republican slate, while New York Assemblyman Luis Nine, a Puerto Rican from Mayagüez, was Cunningham's candidate for the Democrats. Fortunately, my constituents figured out what had happened and knew the story. I was popular in the churches (and synagogues), the party and the neighborhood. They knew how to play the game, and I think actually enjoyed the intrigue.

The polls closed at 9 p.m. Half an hour later, Tony Burgos called me at home. He'd worked for me when I was state senator and was now serving as my campaign manager.

"We're winning by a landslide! Come on over!"

Both Tony and Marlene Cintrón were great organizers and had helped make my victory happen. They'd rented a local eatery for that night, hoping it would be for a celebration . . . and it was a great night! A huge mass of people turned out, really incredible in my eyes.

The next day, however, started out as something of a downer. We had won the election, and now the real work would begin. It was a typically cold February day, and I was sitting at home mulling it all over, solitary in my one-bedroom apartment on 149th Street in the South Bronx. The excitement of being surrounded by my supporters had cooled down for the moment. My wife Anita and I had separated, and that was on my mind as well. I'd called her to see if maybe we could try to make our marriage work again, and she agreed to go with me to my swearing-in ceremony. That was a difficult, emotional time, and I was trying to do this more for the children, since she and I had really drifted apart.

I was considering what would come next. My two boys were young men: Robert starting as a freshman at American University in Washington, DC and Kenneth finishing high school. They both had good character, and I admired their fortitude, the way they carried themselves. My adopted daughter Rozzie had married and settled down with her husband and child. I loved all three of my children dearly and was a caring father, but I knew that my political world had taken me away from them on many family occasions. To be a good public servant you have to be just that: being out with the people, seeing what they need, how you can help, talking with your cohorts, horse-trading. That's the way it is, always on the go. You have to make your choices in life, and that had been mine. But it hadn't been easy on the family.

Then the phone rang that dreary day, interrupting my depressing thoughts about how volatile life was: one minute surrounded by admirers, the next moment all alone. It was the first call of many I'd receive that day. Phil Burton, the chair of the Democratic Caucus, was on the line to congratulate me. Since I was just beginning and he was a very important, long-time congressman from San Francisco (one of the old-time, savvy liberal Democrats who wielded a lot of power), his call was an honor. It surprised me to hear from him, because it really hadn't sunk in as to how much power a congressman had. I'd never been a big-shot power guy like Badillo. That was just not me—never has been—even though the attraction to politics was very real. I loved getting into things to see that they'd be done right, helping resolve problems, being in the midst of important decisions and growing in self-confidence. To be a player at the beginning of Hispanic empowerment during the civil rights movement had been exhilarating. And there was more to come.

Burton greeted me effusively on the phone. "Welcome!" he said. "Come see me as soon as you come to town, and we'll decide which committees are open, where you want to serve. We're happy you're joining us."

Bruce Caputo, a Republican from Yonkers, called me later that day too and said I should join *their* caucus, but I clarified that I was a Democrat! I thanked him for the invite, though. They had surely helped by putting me on the ticket, but that was not where my lifelong loyalties lay.

Going from being part of a minority in the state senate, even becoming the chair of my party there, to becoming part of the majority party in the US House of Representatives would mean a world of difference. I'd be where the action was and hoped I'd be able to really get things done. The Hispanics still needed to integrate the Civil Rights Act into their own communities. New York City was on the verge of bankruptcy. Decent housing for the poor was virtually nonexistent. There was so much work that needed to be done, and it was thrilling for me to realize that I'd be part of it.

The Democratic Caucus and Committees

A few days later, I was on my way to National Airport, with old, scuffed shoes and all. *The New York Times* would later say, and quite correctly, that my new wife Jane was the one who taught me how to get my hair cut, dress better and keep my shoes shined. Maybe the report was right. Maybe I wasn't the best-dressed man to hit town that session, but I was there. I'd been tempered by the Bronx streets, the Korean War, the New York legislature, the civil rights movement, Attica and prison reform. I knew where I was and where I wanted to go. That was the key.

I'd taken the shuttle down to Washington, DC often enough, but this time was very different, now that I was an elected representative to the 95th Congress. I remember it so well. It was a beautiful, sunny day. The view out the airplane porthole was spectacular. I clearly saw, one by one, the Capitol, the Washington Monument and the Lincoln Memorial as though looking at them for the first time. I'll never forget that moment, the physical thrill and adrenaline of beginning a new life. The challenge and prospect of representing my district in the nation's capital moved me as nothing had ever before.

First, I checked in with Anita at the Hyatt, where we stayed for a few days. After I was sworn in, she returned to New York, and I moved in with my friend Nelson Díaz's family. I didn't feel like I was imposing because Nelson was, after all, the one who encouraged me to run for the seat. His offer seemed to be a repeat of the hospitality Nuyoricans offered newcomers from the island. Díaz and I were lifelong friends.

Once in DC, I soon caught what's called "Potomac Fever." It's hard to resist. Entering the heady world of the nation's capital can be as unnerving as it is as exhilarating. Imagine being one of that select group of individuals—one of 535 men and women in the Senate and the House—elected by their peers in their hometowns to go to Washington, DC to study, debate and pass laws that affect the entire country and that reverberate throughout the globe. You'd have to serve on committees and become experts in everything from national park lands to foreign aid. And in two short years, you'd have to stand for reelection, resulting in an incredibly difficult balancing act, a challenging intellectual and human relations exercise. Plus, you'd be courted by many for your influence within the government and its bureaucracy. It's nothing new. That's been the way it has been dating back to President George Washington.

The United States of America is the wealthiest, most powerful government on the face of the Earth. Its democratic and republican form of government works under the most demanding set of rules and scrutiny and competition imaginable. Just as no one can really ever be prepared to be president of the United States, to a lesser extent no one can really prepare to be a member of the House of Representatives. But it surely helps if one has served in the legislature at the state level, as I did, for many years, learning to know and serve one's constituents well. Another advantage is the ability to choose the most capable staff. I was able to call on some good people who had worked with me through the years in New York. Even so, they were, as was I, new to the national scene. It would be a new set of protocols and responsibilities.

I quickly went over to my new office on the seventh floor of the Longworth Building, which needed to be fixed up a little for my new DC-based staff and me. We'd set up my office, and I'd be ready to go.

There were thirty-nine congressmen from New York, more than any other state, as it was still number one in population in 1978. But only two of us had emerged in the special election: Bill Green and me. Bill, a Republican representing the financially powerful "silk-stocking" district, had won a stunning upset over the flamboyant and popular Democrat Bella Abzug. Everyone on the national scene knew her because of her big hats and bigger personality, but Bella had lost to Bill. Then I, openly a Democrat, had run as a Republican. One way or the other, all 435 of us congressmen would have to run again in eight months in the regular general election.

New York Senators Daniel Patrick Moynihan and Jacob Javits escorted Bill and me to the Well, the center of activity in the House chamber. The chamber had been renovated in the early 1950s, with the entire ceiling redone, including a perimeter featuring plaster reliefs of the state and territory seals. Above the Well, directly above the president during his annual State of the Union address, was the seal of Puerto Rico, not in some corner, but in a truly special place.

It was in the Well that we were sworn in by Speaker of the House Tip O'Neill, that burly, effective—sometimes charming and always tough—fellow Democrat from Massachusetts. He knew how to get things done. He was a great example of how politicians in DC should work and of a politician who knew how to cross the aisle for the good of the American people. After taking the oath to defend the

Constitution, I was directed to Phil Burton's office to get my credentials with the Democratic Party Caucus. Because I had won as a Republican, I had to go back and rectify my party standing. There was no problem with that on either side, and we hit it off as well in person as we had on the phone that first day after my election. We talked about a little of everything, and he assigned me the committees I asked for.

Again, this was an emotional time for me. Anita returned to New York, still unsure of our future together, although we were now more frequently talking divorce. Despite my emotions, I went forward in my political life. I had made that life choice.

Only a few days after I'd been sworn in, President Jimmy Carter invited me to the White House alone. Back then, it was standard operating procedure for the president to invite newly elected members of Congress of his political party to a one-on-one courtesy meeting. There I was in the Oval Office, in awe of the trappings of power of the most powerful leader in the world, in the presence of the man who led the Democratic Party power base. President Carter was quite friendly and rather informal in manner. Of course, there was no doubt who held the power. After all, besides being an ex-governor of Georgia, Carter had been a Navy officer who'd trained under the famed Admiral Hyman G. Rickover. He knew how to exercise authority.

As I was leaving the office, he asked me to vote against pending legislation for the B-1 bomber. Of course, I agreed. Walking out, I thought, "Wow! The first time I've been lobbied as a congressman, and it's by the president of our country!"

Advancing Civil Rights for Hispanics

In the US House of Representatives, the House Democratic Caucus includes a Steering and Policy Committee when the Democrats are in the majority. Its primary purpose is to assign party members to the House committees. The newly elected members of Congress try to get on the committees that have a direct bearing on their own congressional districts. Members of this committee are the leadership of the party as well as designated representatives of twelve various regions around the country.

In 1982 I was selected by the New York Democratic delegation to serve as their representative on Steering and Policy Committee. When the members who were elected in 1982 arrived in Washington, DC, their first order of business was to lobby the individual members who would be on the committee to assign them to the committees they wanted. We'd try to satisfy the new members whenever possible. Of course, to get on the most sought-after committees, such as Ways and Means, Appropriations, Rules or Energy and Commerce, was particularly difficult, and many members with seniority often wanted to be promoted to those committees. When we gathered for the first time to start making our appointments of the new members, I found myself in a situation where not only was I trying to make certain that New York members got what they were looking for, but also that the five new Hispanics became part of the newly created Congressional Hispanic Caucus. As chairman of the caucus, I also had the responsibility of making certain that the five new Hispanics coming into Congress were assigned to committees they were satisfied with and that would help them in their districts.

Bill Richardson was among the five members who joined the House in early 1983 and was looking to become a member of the Commerce and Energy Committee, knowing that it would be helpful to his New Mexico district. But it was also a committee that had quite a few other applicants, some with seniority. I placed Bill Richardson's name in nomination for Energy and Commerce, and immediately Charlie Wilson of oil-rich East Texas objected. There was then a rather heavy discussion between Wilson and me, which ended with me asking Wilson to meet with Richardson to see if we could iron out what his problems were. Unbeknownst to me at the start, it soon became clear that Wilson's problem lay in the fact that East Texas was an oil-drilling part of the state, and Charlie was unsure how Bill Richardson would vote on the issues dealing with oil. Obviously, I could not answer that question. After the two of them talked, Wilson got back to me and gave the go-ahead to place Bill Richardson on Energy and Commerce. As it turned out, Bill did support Wilson on certain energy issues that affected East Texas, but not all.

The story of how congressmen get to be placed first on full committees and then on sub-committees, and how it works from there, with hearings, drafting legislation, the floor debates and all provides an interesting look at the inner workings of Congress. I was fortunate in having experienced the same sort of protocol in the New York Senate, because it's not an easy task to master. It's a kind of mini-civics orientation about the House of Representatives in action. Each committee had anywhere from three to six subcommittees under the full committee.

I chose the Banking, Housing and Urban Affairs Committee even though banking is surely not my forte; my inability to balance my personal checkbooks would become public knowledge years later. Banking was definitely not my *shtick*, but safe housing surely was. Mayor Ed Koch would need my support to ensure funding for new public housing for New York City to rebuild blighted areas, such as the South Bronx, which by now looked like it had been bombed as the result of riots, fires and general decay. Among the Banking sub-committees, the one on housing would handle any loans to New York City, very important for an urban center teetering on the edge of bankruptcy. That year, 1978, was crucial for New York City and the Bronx.

Years later, in 2012, I drove and walked all through my old neighborhood. It had been revitalized, worlds beyond what it had been before. It was federal dollars, paid by taxpayers from all over the United States, that had made its rebirth from the ashes possible. Looking back on it, I'm amazed how I, this street-smart kid from the Bronx, could so quickly adapt well to the rhythm of Congress.

The Civil Service Reform Bill, "Hispanic" added to the Census and the Garcia Amendment

Another, and just as important, area was the role of Hispanics in national life. Phil Burton named me to the Post Office and Civil Service Committee, and then its Sub-Committee on Census and

Population. Both could be significant in seeing minorities fairly represented in public service and federal programs. The Post Office and Civil Service Committee would be important in reforming Civil Service and opening the door to qualified Hispanics and other minorities. At that time Hispanics and other minorities were incredibly underrepresented throughout the nation's Civil Service, even though there were many fully qualified people available. The situation was, in great part, a matter of communication: information about upcoming Civil Service exams was held close to the vest and, by the time the minorities heard about them, the exams had been given and jobs were offered. Minorities were effectively shut out.

The Sub-Committee on Census and Population was under the full Post Office and Civil Service Committee. Though not a highly visible post, I wanted it because I knew the leverage it would give Hispanics throughout the nation in future elections. If we weren't even counted, we wouldn't have as many district representatives as we were entitled to. The upcoming 1980 census would be extremely important for Hispanics throughout the whole country; it could give us more of a say in Congress and at all levels of government: municipal, county, state, local school boards and so on. It would be a very big deal, as Hispanics had traditionally been undercounted in previous census-taking. I never expected to be the chair of that sub-committee, but the very next year I was elected to head it.

President Carter's presidential campaign had stressed the need to reform the Civil Service. The nominal head of the Post Office and Civil Service Committee was Robert Nix, a Democrat from Philadelphia. But the real driving force was Mo Udall, the congressman from Arizona, with whom I had a good relationship. He was a giant of a man, both physically and in terms of character. He was a dynamic yet unassuming person, with great wit and smarts, and he'd be leading the charge for the Reform Act.

In the Democratic presidential primaries, I had successfully run as a Udall delegate from Manhattan's East Side, something that then qualified me to go to the 1976 Democratic Convention in New York's Madison Square Garden. When Udall didn't have the votes to win the nomination, he released his delegates to vote for Jimmy Carter as the party's candidate for president. Carter won the election in November, beating incumbent Republican President Gerald R. Ford, who had stepped into the presidency after Nixon resigned because of the Watergate scandal.

I accompanied Mo and other members of Congress to meet with President Carter at the White House to discuss the language that could go into the legislation required to reform the Federal Civil Service and other matters. I was just three weeks into my new job as a member of Congress and once again found myself sitting with the president of the United States! Only in America!

All five of us Hispanics in the meeting took advantage of the opportunity to discuss a variety of issues. Each of us made a statement. When it was the turn of Baltasar Corrada del Río, the resident commissioner from Puerto Rico (who had a non-voting seat on the floor in Congress) to speak, he started reading something aloud. I thought, why was he was wasting this meeting with the president of the United States to read a document?! Baltasar was a renowned lawyer in San Juan but had apparently become inarticulate at that moment. We would later see that "Balta," as we called him, could be quite verbal and even got into a tiff on the floor of Congress. After everyone had spoken and we had discussed the business on the agenda, President Carter, an ardent defender of civil rights, asked if there was anything else.

I took the opportunity to say, "The census has never reflected the real number of Hispanics in America. Many Hispanics are mixed-race and don't want to identify as white, Black and certainly not as 'other.' It's very important we finally have an accurate count in the 1980 census."

President Carter not only listened but acted. How important it is to have good communication between the chief executive and the legislature! After hearing about my determination to ensure that Hispanics would be properly counted in the upcoming census, the president issued an executive order: for the first time, the word "Hispanic" would appear as an option in the "Race" section on the 1980 census form. It was a small but all-important step toward recognition. The census-takers would now be aware of the need to seek out everyone, and Hispanics—that huge group of Spanish-speakers and inheritors of Latino culture—would finally and massively demonstrate our presence in the United States.

Following up on this, just a few days later, President Carter sent me a copy of the notes he'd jotted down in our meeting on a pad with "WH" at the top. He had written just a few lines, "Dear Juanita, Congressman Garcia is concerned about the correct count of Hispanics. Jimmy," and sent the message to Juanita Krebs, Secretary of Commerce, who was in charge of the census program. It was her job to administer the program, and Congress' job to make sure everything went smoothly and that there was sufficient funding. It was a sign of courtesy that he'd sent me a copy and was following up on the matter. It was interesting to see he'd signed it simply, "Jimmy," instead of with his initials.

I was especially happy to be involved with the Civil Service Reform group in Congress, as I had served many years on the NY State Senate Labor Committee, which dealt with the appointment of state employees to civil service. For years I'd battled to open the doors of opportunity for qualified minorities, but try as I might, I kept hitting a stone wall of Republican opposition. When we held a three-day Black and Hispanic Legislative Conference, I was chair of the Labor Committee and used that position to make a great point about the need for this type of law. But there was no budging the Republicans in Albany. The state was happy with the system and rejected change.

Back then, there were few minorities in government, either at the state or federal levels. It's important to mention that in no way was that legislation aimed at creating job quotas or promoting unmerited hiring. Everyone had to take the entrance exams and pass them. What it did do, however, was finally make the playing field level. Within months of being in Congress, I presented what became known as the "Garcia Bill" to ensure that qualified Hispanics and minorities were correctly represented, that they would be properly informed, and on time, about Civil Service exam schedules and that they'd be considered on an equal footing with everyone else seeking to enter public service. Now in Congress, and suddenly part of the majority party, I could get things done. In retrospect I am proud that as a junior congressman with only months under my belt I was able to achieve an important step forward for minorities.

To become law, bills being considered by Congress must go through conferences between both bodies to iron-out any differences that may have arisen between their respective versions. A commission is formed with members of both the House and the Senate to craft a compromise bill. Then each body must approve the compromise bill before a final version is sent to the president for his signature. Each step is important. After coming out of the conference committee, the bill included the amended language I'd introduced, which stated that everyone should be notified about Civil Service exams and that qualified Hispanics and minorities should be represented according to their population in hiring. Senator Arlen Specter (R-Pennsylvania) argued that I was asking for quotas, but I said no, we were talking only about those who qualified. The chair, Senator Abraham Ribicoff (D-Connecticut), agreed and cut off the debate. The fact that Mo Udall was a conference member helped ensure that my amendment would sail through.

It was voted on and passed by the full Congress. President Carter signed the Civil Service Reform Act of 1978, now including the "Garcia Bill." When President Reagan assumed office, he simply ignored it, but left it on the books.

NATO

Congressman Phil Burton called me one fine day after I was installed as a freshman congressman and summarily informed me: "I want you on my committee to oversee NATO, the sixteen-nation North Atlantic Treaty Organization, as a standing member of the official US delegation. We leave in four or five days for a meeting in Brussels. I want you there."

This was an important international post, in the years before the fall of the Berlin Wall; the Cold War was still raging. There were no ifs, ands or buts I could offer.

"Europeans need to understand urban America," he went on, "and I can think of no better example than you to make them understand. These guys need to know about inner cities, minorities, immigration . . . the whole nine yards."

I accepted, and it was one of the best decisions I ever made. It resulted in me getting a broad exposure to the way the world really works.

On that first trip, I was seated next to Baltasar Corrada del Río, Puerto Rico's elected resident commissioner. It was the usual military-type plane used to shuttle congressmen: no windows, seats pretty close together. I'm a big guy, and even though I was an athlete back in the day, I can be clumsy in small places. Anyway, I spilled coffee on him; he got angry but eventually simmered down. We got along well together after that incident. Balta was a good guy, very smart with a highly legalistic way of seeing things. He usually measured his words with an innate sweet manner. He was honest. He spoke English with a pronounced Puerto Rican accent. And equally important as all the above . . . he was a Democrat.

That first trip to Brussels was my first visit to Europe. When I arrived in the city, I looked around and thought, "What am I doing in international politics, this boy from the South Bronx?" I heard myself answer my own question: "We in the South Bronx are as capable as anyone else. I'll just be aware of others, listen, analyze and work hard." I was full of energy and exhilarated with all those new challenges.

Once in Brussels, I signed on as part of the Civilian Affairs Committee of NATO. I was neither political nor military but involved with my own abiding interests in human rights, Radio Free Europe and so on. I was soon elected chair of that committee by my fellow members.

Surrounded by military brass and politicians from North America and Europe, I soon realized that politicians are politicians are politicians, no matter where they're from! In our respective democratic states, we all respond to our electorate. Our jobs are pretty much alike. I learned that the people from the United Kingdom, France, Denmark and the United States all had much more in common than not. In spite of language and cultural differences, and different government procedures, we still had the same motivation: to serve our countries to the best of our abilities and to be accountable in our work. In working together, we also learned that personalities and character were important in our relationships, just as they were back home.

Mell Metson, the representative from Denmark would become my friend and staunch ally. Stunningly beautiful and sweet in nature, she had chaired the Civilian Affairs Committee before me. Mell was always helpful to me, the novice from America. I remember once I started sermonizing about human rights violations in Nicaragua, and she graciously turned the discussion another way. At the same time, I remembered, "Good Lord! This is NATO, not Latin America! Slow down!" I guess it was due to the fact that at I was already very much involved in congressional oversight on protecting human rights in Central and South America.

Working in NATO was a truly great experience. At that time, we had several European film crews filming unflattering documentaries and Hollywood movies, such as *Fort Apache, The Bronx*. I wanted the world to know, through the influential people in NATO, that the South Bronx was not really like the hellhole portrayed in the movie. Neither was all the news that focused only on the devastation, fire-bombed buildings and the urban poor. I invited the European parliamentarians by the dozen to visit the Bronx. When they took me up on the invitation, I took them everywhere on chartered buses—to churches, schools and community organizations—to meet ordinary people, government and private businesses, all working together to reclaim the South Bronx that was my home and my pride.

As part of that NATO experience, which lasted for twelve years, I chaired the Committee on Civilian Affairs, dealing with international issues affecting human rights, education and cultural affairs. It was actually NATO's only non-political or non-military committee, which was why it was the only one I wanted. It dealt with a broad spectrum of issues involving the new problems facing Europe, including immigration from former African, Caribbean and Middle Eastern colonies. But the Cold War with the USSR was still frigid, and our biggest concern as Americans was keeping Radio Free Europe alive and well. This was before the internet, so Radio Free

Europe was our best tool to reach behind the Iron Curtain to places where freedom did not ring. Once in Portugal and again in Munich, Jane and I visited the towers that transmitted Radio Free Europe's vital programs and their democratic messages of hope to all the European countries under Communist domination. I could envision people listening to our messages on clandestine radios and dreaming of democracy.

I was especially happy to serve in NATO because we made life-long friends in many countries. This was possible because we had many common denominators, despite our different languages and cultures; just getting to know the problems of a country through these friendships made decisions much more workable in our committee meetings.

The Panama Canal Treaty

A couple of months after I'd been in office, I was asked to meet with President Carter in the Cabinet Room to discuss a new Panama Canal accord to replace the United States' ninety-nine-year lease on the Canal Zone. He wanted to discuss some of the problems he was facing in enacting the new treaty. Mo Udall was the leader of the initiative in Congress. Udall, as I pointed out earlier, had run a strong, but unsuccessful, campaign against Carter for the Democratic nomination for president, but there was no residual rancor. In fact, Mo had given the introductory speech for the nomination of Jimmy Carter as president at the convention.

Some have criticized President Carter for micro-managing the Executive Branch instead of working closely enough with Congress and for being indecisive as the country's chief executive. I could never say that. He was open, honest, decisive and passionate about civil rights. I'm sure that's one of the reasons he paid some attention to me, because as Hispanic I represented a minority that has been subject to discrimination. In my opinion, his stance on civil rights and personal integrity overshadowed what others might have seen as flaws.

Three people in the Senate, two Democrats and one Republican, gave us a hard time on Panama. Senator Dennis DiConcini, a Republican from Arizona and a powerful leader, was dead set against it. Knowing this, Mo Udall gave me a call: "Would you agree to our drawing up a press release, to be signed by the Hispanics in Congress, saying the Hispanic Caucus strongly backs the Panama Canal Treaty? We could release the news on the weekend, only in Arizona, and see if that budges him."

I agreed, and the other Hispanics in the House also agreed. The press release went out in the senator's home state and, sure enough, he quickly changed his mind. He depended on his state's Hispanic votes. It was a little lesson in the clout we now possessed and how we could use it again in the future.

President Jimmy Carter pushed through the new treaty with Panama, relinquishing control of the Canal Zone. But there were many details to work out.

In deference to my being Hispanic, Carter invited me to go with him and others to Panama to sign the treaty with President (and virtual dictator) Omar Torrijos. It was an enlightening visit in many ways.

It was September 7, 1977, when we were all standing on a balcony overlooking a huge plaza. Thousands of Panamanians cheered and yelled in an enormous uproar. I thought the cheering would never stop. Then Torrijos, after saluting the crowd, raised his index finger to his lips in a "hush" motion. The crowd's roar stopped immediately. I mean immediately! Not a whisper could be heard.

I said to myself, watching this man in action, "What incredible power!" I had never before, nor since, seen that kind of crowd response and obedience. It was truly impressive, if not a bit scary.

China

In 1979, on one of my visits to the Far East as a member of the Congressional Banking Committee, we went to China, Japan and Thailand. When we were taking off from Andrews Airforce Base, President Carter called Representative Lud Ashley, the congressman from Ohio and chair of our committee to request that we also take on the role of official US delegation to China following restoration of full diplomatic relations, exchanging ambassadors and all the other protocol. (President Nixon had famously opened the door to Communist China, first by visiting the country and then establishing reciprocal airline routes.)

As we arrived in Beijing, we were suddenly not only a congressional delegation but also representatives of the White House. We were treated royally. In the banquet hall at Tiananmen Square, we were separated and seated throughout the vast dining room to listen to the speeches and watch the festivities with various Chinese dignitaries. I ended up with three or four generals.

After one of the generals had addressed our group, in English, I wanted to return the gesture and mentioned, "You know, in 1952 I was fighting Chinese soldiers in Korea. And yet, now . . . here we are." As soon as the words left my mouth, I got nervous, not knowing what the general would respond. There was silence. After what seemed like an eternity but was probably only three or four seconds, he replied politely, "Ah, but we were enemies then. Now we are friends!" We all laughed and smiled. I've always remembered that moment. . . . Ah, Diplomacy!

Tip O'Neill and Argentina's President Raúl Alfonsín

Prime Minister Margaret Thatcher, Britain's indefatigable "Iron Lady" and a great friend of President Ronald Reagan, was visiting Washington after the Falklands War they had successfully fought with Argentina. At the same time, the Ambassador of Argentina had spoken to me to request that their newly elected President Raúl Alfonsín be allowed to address Congress. I thought it was extremely important since Argentina has gotten rid of its dictatorial military junta and entered the family of democratic nations with a popularly elected president.

I was often involved in mediating matters regarding Latin America because of my own Hispanic background—and okay Spanish, certainly not the florid diplomatic Spanish Jane would use—and in turn, had very good relationships with nearly all the Spanish-speaking ambassadors to the United States. In fact, my wife Jane ended up leading a Bible study group in Spanish for many years at the "Christian Embassy" for the Latin American ambassadors' spouses (and one female ambassador) in Washington, DC.

As a result of the Argentine ambassador's call, I asked Speaker of the House Tip O'Neill to extend that privilege.

He couldn't believe what I was asking, and reflexively answered, "No! Especially not with Margaret Thatcher being here!"

I said, "On the contrary, allowing him to address Congress is proof that we back fellow democratic governments. Since the newly elected president has requested that honor, it would be a terrific blow to their national pride for us to turn them down. And our Hispanic constituents would consider it an insult if they were to find out."

He glared at me with that famous Tip O'Neill glower . . . and didn't say anything else. A short while later, he officially invited President Alfonsín to address Congress.

Meanwhile, on the personal level, my wife Anita and I had irrevocably drifted apart. I kept up with our kids, but she and I simply could not get along anymore. We agreed to make arrangements for a divorce but still hadn't filed for it. By now I had been thoroughly caught up and consumed with passion for my work in Congress. It had become my life. And my relationship with Puerto Rico would become closer than ever, as I was the only voting member of the House of Representatives of Puerto Rican heritage . . . its *de facto* voting congressman.

Politics in Puerto Rico

Since it was and is but a territory of the United States and, notwithstanding the fact that its residents born there are automatically US citizens, Puerto Rico was not impacted by district reapportionment or the census counting for Hispanics to increase its numbers in Congress. Being an unincorporated territory, the island's US citizens do not vote for a representative or a senator. They only have a resident commissioner who may vote in a congressional committee, but not on the floor.

Even so, the census was important for Puerto Rico on many levels: helping allot funding by federal agencies for the island's poor, its infrastructure, roads, security, immigration, federal justice system and so on. We held several hearings in Puerto Rico to bolster interest in the upcoming census and its implementation. One hearing was held in the capital city of San Juan and the other in the island's second-largest city, Ponce.

Baltasar Corrada del Río, whom I've mentioned several times earlier, had served for four years as the resident commissioner and was running for election at the same time as the island's governor. More than our mainland political parties, the island's political status is what really drives Puerto Rican politics, reaching even into Puerto Rican communities in the continental United States. Baltasar was a political liberal and a dedicated Democrat, as was his running mate, Governor Carlos Romero Barceló. But their dedication to statehood for the island via its New Progressive Party was their overriding concern. In 1970, resident Commissioner Jorge Luis Córdova, who identified as a Democrat, ran with the founder of the pro-statehood New Progressive Party, Republican Luís A. Ferré, but switched to identifying as a Republican in DC because of his friendship with House powerhouse Gerald R. Ford. After that, two pro-statehood governors would identify as Democrats: Carlos Romero Barceló, who did so while governor and as resident commissioner after serving as governor; he then became a Republican and served on the Platform Committee of the Republican Party in 1988 and successfully included a plank supporting statehood. The other was Governor Pedro Rosselló, who served from 1993 to 2001. Luis Fortuño, a Republican, was first elected resident commissioner in 2004, then governor in 2008 with a Democratic running mate for resident commissioner, Pedro Pierluisi. Fortuño named another active Democrat, Kenneth McClintock, as Puerto Rico's secretary of state. Thus, the statehood movement has included both Republicans and Democrats, while the *Popular* party has been consistently identified with the Democratic Party on the mainland.

The Independence movement leaders have never endorsed or identified themselves with either national political party.

Puerto Rico's political status, as I mentioned earlier, has always been a passion-inducing subject, first under Spain and then under the United States. One verbal incident on the floor of the House illustrates the neverending controversy. Representative Ron Dellums (Democrat) from Berkeley, California cut an imposing figure. He was tall, elegant—easily the best-dressed man in the House—with a self-assured, articulate and engaging manner. Part of the radical group of northern California black intellectuals—he was a good friend of the well-known Angela Davis and the Black Panthers—he could be as intimidating or charming as he wished, depending on the moment. Representing Oakland, Dellums was a part of an anti-Vietnam War group that played a major role in the early '60s and well into the '70s. As is every congressman's right to do, Dellums circulated a "Dear Colleague" letter to his fellow congressmen, in which he strongly backed independence for Puerto Rico and asked for his fellow members' support. Since the independence movement had been associated with leftists, and Dellums was an avowed socialist, this was a natural . . . no big surprise. Puerto Rico's Resident Commissioner Baltasar Corrada del Río fired back with his own "Dear Colleague" letter, not only backing statehood and vilifying independence, but calling Dellums a Communist. They both were fired up.

I had been sitting in the House when I saw the very tall Dellums come up, loom over Corrada and yell, "You M**F**R, you! What do you mean by calling me a Communist, you M**F**R. Come outside and fight it out!"

"What do you mean?" Baltasar said, leaping to his feet. Usually mild-mannered, he snarled back, in his heavily accented tenor voice, waving his hands. "M**RF**R? *YOU'RE* the M**RF**R!"

They both started shouting, gesticulating wildly at each other and obviously calling a great deal of attention to themselves in the usually placid House chamber. This was right at the front of the House floor, not in some corner, but center stage, right under Puerto Rico's plaster seal on the chamber's ceiling.

Fortunately, I got along with both of them—and I'm a big guy myself—so I went over and like a boxing referee said, "Come on, guys, let's cool it. Come on!"

They glowered at each other but stopped for a moment and looked at me.

"Let's meet in my office tomorrow at noon, and you can sort this out, okay? Calm down now."

They reluctantly nodded agreement and parted ways.

True to their word, the next day they both showed up at my office at noon, sharp. I showed them in, closed the door and left. The secret to mediation is to let the opposing sides talk to each other in a private, neutral and non-threatening atmosphere. Obviously, they were able to make peace because, when I came back a half hour later, there was no blood on the floor! And they both were being civil to each other after the explosive incident.

I'll never forget it, though: Baltasar talking like that in public. He was always so gentlemanly, courteous and formal in his manner. He was from a large family in the Puerto Rican countryside, had one brother who was a bishop and a sister who was a nun, both of them strong independence-backers. I'm sure Balta had had plenty of opportunities to discuss politics with his siblings, but I really doubt their discussions ever devolved to four- or six-letter words! But such are the emotions that "status," the political relationship between the federal government and Puerto Rico, continue to provoke a century after those born on the island were made US citizens . . . second-class citizens. . . .

CHAPTER SIX

Jane

Puerto Rico loomed large in my vision. This was a natural, not only because of my own background, but also because so many of my constituents were continually traveling back forth from the island to the continental United States, not only to New York City. But as a thoroughly urban creature, to me New York was surely the hub of the Puerto Rican continental community. My heart and home were always centered squarely in New York, and of course the Bronx. However, by default I was rapidly gaining the reputation in Congress among my peers as "Mr. Puerto Rico." The reason was that without a voting member representing the island, I got a constant stream of people from Puerto Rico, from mayors of towns to bank presidents, medical professionals representing hospitals, CEOs of huge pharmaceutical conglomerates, the Puerto Rico Chamber of Commerce and university presidents filing through my office with requests to amend pending legislation to specifically include Puerto Rico, or the island and its citizens would be left out. Since each federal agency treated Puerto Rico arbitrarily according to its own independent dictates, each separate agency decided how much to allot to the island Medicare, food stamps, educational apportionments. . . . Everything had to be addressed legislatively. In every administration, no matter what party was in power in Puerto Rico, I was asked by the governor, the head of his office for federal affairs in DC or the resident commissioner to help with one thing or another, and I always did. My concern was the Puerto Rican people, and so it was my policy to work with all comers in all administrations, following my heart and conscience to determine if the requests were good for the people.

When Baltasar Corrada del Río was the resident commissioner, he would lobby me on behalf of many special interests concerning Puerto Rico, especially in areas of health, education, housing and security. In the course of this traffic of requests coming from Puerto Rico, early on I met José "Pepe" Méndez, a Puerto Rican educator who was an incredibly effective entrepreneur in higher education. He was frequently in DC looking for educational grants and federal allocations; he expertly used those resources to build an educational empire. He was the kind of person you helped eagerly and who delivered tangible results for the community. Pepe was the son of educational pioneer Ana G. Méndez; he took his mother's small junior college, which she'd originally started as a secretarial school in Río Piedras, Puerto Rico, and turned it into a dynamo known today as the Ana G. Méndez University System. At first it filled the need for community colleges, which the public university system sorely lacked. Pepe eventually turned the colleges into an island-wide university system that focused on both two-year associate degrees and career-aimed education. It became a much-needed resource, filling a void in Puerto Rico and then became incredibly successful in expanding to the Dominican Republic. Next it opened campuses at several locations in the continental United States, the most recent in Maryland. Those resources made educational opportunities available for Hispanics from every part of Latin America and the United States, offering scholarships and grants in many fields.

In June 1979, Pepe invited me to Puerto Rico to give the commencement speech at the Inter-American University. I readily accepted and didn't think twice about asking him if it was expected to be in English; I just assumed. I arrived two days early, to visit some friends in government to see how I could help Puerto Rico in Congress. I went to see Doel García, an old crony from my New York senate days who was serving at the time as the director of tourism in Governor Romero Barceló's administration. Tourism was key to the island's economy and was beginning to thrive right about then with the advertising campaign, "Puerto Rico, USA". This was a clever marketing strategy because it told people they didn't have to get vaccinations and passports to travel. The Ana G. Méndez group, with its usual astuteness, jumped on the bandwagon and offered associate degrees related to the tourism industry. Thus, the invitation to be the keynote speaker at that year's graduation in San Juan was related to this push for tourism.

It was during this trip that my friend Doel recommended that I meet a young, savvy, Puerto Rican woman who was moving to Washington, DC that next month. He had planned to hire her himself for a dream he'd long had of opening an office in DC to channel conventions to the island as part of his tourism efforts. He didn't have the approved budget just yet but thought that in the meantime she'd be a great addition to my congressional staff. Not only was she smart, aggressive and organized, he assured me, but she was trilingual and well-connected in Puerto Rico. Jane Lee Matos was her name.

Doel set up a meeting with her in my hotel lobby, and—BAM!— this vibrant, gorgeous young woman walked into my life. And she has stayed there ever since. I can never forget the great electric shock that coursed through me on meeting her. It was like a bolt of lightning! I was blown away by her absolutely stunning looks and self-assured presence. This was a cosmopolitan woman, brimming with energy and know-how. The combination was something I had never encountered, and I was instantly smitten.

We sat down tentatively on a lobby sofa and, after a short conversation and a cursory look at her resume, I asked her to join me for an end-of-a-long-day cocktail. I could see her hesitancy; she probably thought it wasn't such a good idea but accepted and smiled up at me as I took her arm and escorted her to the bar. Before the waiter arrived with the drinks, I not only offered her the job, but began a relentless, hot pursuit of Jane. I was leaving the next morning and wanted to pin down when I could expect her to arrive in DC. We agreed to meet in Miami, where I would be in mid-June to conduct a census hearing. I invited her to come and get an idea of the work she would be involved in. That conveniently coincided with her planned trip to Florida at school year's end to take her daughters to stay with her mother Christina for the summer, while she organized her life as a new divorcee. I, of course, was already separated from my wife.

She told me her brother Alex was living in DC, having just completed his Masters in International Affairs at Johns Hopkins University. It was he who had encouraged his older sister to come look around Washington, DC and had even arranged for her to look at places to stay and schools for her two girls.

Everything was a fit!

I tell her story here partially because she gave me a deeper understanding of the people on the island of Puerto Rico, whom I had not had any real encounter with, nor any previous real knowledge of. Frankly, the Puerto Ricans I knew were mostly like me. Most came from migrant parents and most were poor. Jane came from a different, more economically advantaged class in Puerto Rico: well-established, well-educated, well-mannered and refined. I think it's important to show both sides of the coin and establish the difference in our backgrounds, to get the full story going forward.

Jane had left her husband after a turbulent marriage of fourteen years. She was in the midst of divorcing him and fleeing to the mainland. It was a sad and difficult decision for Jane, as she felt he wouldn't be able to take care of himself. She especially hated leaving their beautiful home, the model farm she had built with him over the years, the horses she had literally midwifed and watched develop, not to mention her own horses and the riding and training facilities she had built from scratch. An accomplished horsewoman, she had worked hard with him in developing the Potrero Matos in Guayama, Puerto Rico, an internationally known thoroughbred farm that was written about in such trade magazines as the *Thoroughbred Record* and *Blood Horse*.

She knew in her heart she could do no more; that chapter of her life had ended. It was very heartbreaking. Her two older sons, Robert and Edward, were already in college and the Marines, respectively, while daughters Caroline, 15, and Kirsten, 11, would be spending the summer with Jane's mother in Florida. She had finally decided to take her children and leave the island.

Almost as soon as she arrived in Washington, DC she began to work with me as staff assistant on my congressional Sub-Committee on the Census and Population, where her very real administrative skills quickly became obvious. That was where the most action was, and she helped organize many of the field hearings in the Hispanic and minority areas of the United States and Puerto Rico. The island population was already almost four million but had never been a part of the official census. I wanted to change that.

Then she came to the South Bronx one long weekend to check me out on my own turf. So did her younger brother Alex, who passed his civil service exam and eventually went on to become an assistant deputy secretary of state for Western Hemisphere Affairs. He was a young guy then, just out of school, and he gave me the okay, too. The rest, as they say, is history.

I told my estranged wife that I was in love with this woman and that we both had to move on. She, as well as some of my old friends in the South Bronx, had trouble accepting my decision, but after a difficult few months, our divorce finally went through. Three months later, Jane and I got an apartment on Cathedral Avenue in Northwest, DC. We married while the ink was still wet on both our divorce decrees, but at least they were final, and we eventually moved into an apartment in the South Bronx as our required legal address and primary home, along with the apartment in DC. We worked out of both offices, in the Bronx and in DC. Jane worked mostly in Washington, DC first as part of the census sub-committee and then as administrative assistant on my full staff.

I had always had loyal people around me, but with Jane I felt I had a real partner for the first time, bringing a level of knowledge and sophistication that surely aided my success in Congress. What I really appreciated, beyond her organizational abilities, was her perfect combination of the best of both American and Puerto Rican cultures.

Despite the divorce, my children from my first marriage— Robert, Kenny and Rozzie—and I had, and still have, a good relationship. Some of my friends in the Bronx were unhappy with my new life, but most eventually seemed to realize that each of us follows his own destiny. Jane was a big part of mine.

Jane became very active in the Bronx community, working directly with my constituents, especially in the arts and education, and would eventually hold the position of chair of the board of the Bronx Museum of the Arts for many years, taking this citywide institution to a new level of development. And she stepped naturally into a position as a leader with the Hispanics in DC; on the national level she effortlessly shifted between Cubans, Mexicans, Puerto Ricans and all the Hispanic groups with equal ease and an absolute commitment to all the causes I was involved in. We worked as one and it was, and is, the essence of our happiness together. We both filled a void in the other and felt whole. The voters would show their approval by continuing to elect me as their representative in overwhelming numbers.

Since our marriage, Jane has been a vitally important part of my life both personally and politically. As I grew to know her well, now together for over thirty-five years, I learned of her own family history. A fascinating blend of Anglo and Hispanic cultures, and she's pure Puerto Rican.

Her paternal great-grandfather was Puerto Rico's first playwright, a distinguished man of letters and noted historian: Alejandro Tapia y Rivera (1826–1882). The Tapia Theatre in Old San Juan is named after him. Her grandfather, Albert Edward Lee, married to Tapia's youngest daughter Catalina, was of wealthy entrepreneurial English stock but was born in the same south coast city of Ponce where my mother grew up. The Lee family moved in the island's elite social circles and summered at their mountain estate in Barranquitas, hosting Governor Luis Muñoz Marín and his intimates in the high echelons of politics and class in the mid-twentieth century. Jane's mother Christina was the daughter of a Danish merchant sea-captain and a southern US mother; she was born near New Orleans in the tiny seaport community of Gulfport, Mississippi. Her father disappeared at sea and her mother remarried another man, William B. Creary, who was the president of Bull Lines and the Waterman Steamship business that came to Puerto Rico to develop it as the crossroads of the Americas in shipping. She arrived with her parents and two siblings in Puerto Rico at the age of fourteen and graduated from Central High School in San Juan. She met and married Edward Alexander Lee at a party at the home of Judge Henri Brown. The first six years of their marriage were spent living in San Juan, with summers in Barranquitas. But this happiness was not to be. When her husband Edward developed tuberculosis, there were no hospitals nor sanitariums in Puerto Rico to treat him. This disease was rampant among the poor, especially among the dock workers, where Edward went every day for his family's import-export business, Albert E. Lee and Sons, better known as Casa Lee. At that time, despite the improvements in public health brought by the Americans early in the century, there was only a very limited sanatorium of sorts, mainly for indigents, and it was at full capacity.

Grandfather "Dad" Lee had lived with Edward and Christina after his wife died, creating a special bond; he made it possible for Edward and the family to relocate near a well-known sanatorium in Colorado Springs, Colorado. It was during this period, following a long confinement but still under medical supervision and regimen, that they lived together in the shadow of Pike's Peak. Jane was conceived there, six years after their marriage, and was born at Beth El Hospital in Colorado Springs and baptized Jane Harrison Lee, the Harrison being from her maternal grandmother Jessie Bond Brice, who was not only a Daughter of the American Revolution but a descendant of both Presidents Harrison (9th and 23rd), who were uncle and nephew.

Jane was about forty days old when she arrived in San Juan, where she lived the first seven years of her life. Christina soon realized that she was in for a long haul with Edward's TB, as he relapsed again and again, and she had to park Jane at times with her godmothers, at times with her aunt Consuelo, at times with her maternal grandmother living in Coral Gables, Florida. Christina moved Jane from one place to the next for months at a time while nursing her very ill husband. Eventually when Jane was seven and in second grade at St. John's School, they moved to Switzerland, where they lived the next four years. There, Jane attended an English boarding school as a precaution, because her parents feared exposing her to TB. In children, it could attack the bones, leaving them permanently crippled. At the time, Jane did not understand or appreciate the reason for the long separations, boarding schools and summer camps that kept her apart from her parents and home; she yearned for the warmth of her island home, the people, the food. Today she believes that it made her a survivor in all situations and gave her the inner strength and tenacity that has served her well.

Jane learned to speak French and was exposed at an early age to different cultures and customs, as her school was a home to many privileged children from all over the world. This in turn gave her an ease with people of all races, social classes, creeds and religions. It was in Montreux that she fell in love with horses. Her mother was encouraged by friends to have her learn to ride; equestrianship was almost compulsory for her social class. She took Jane to a nearby riding academy and they both enrolled in a weekly class. By the end of that first summer, it was a daily part of Jane's life and her passion to this day.

Once her father had improved, the family moved back to Puerto Rico. Jane, now ten, returned to St. John's, but her real joy was weekends and summers up in Barranquitas. That was the happiest part of her childhood: her family reunited. Her father was still in delicate health, and the cooler mountain air was a requirement for his full recovery. Christina was in her glory, transforming fifteen acres of land into a garden with fish and lily ponds, imported magnolias and azaleas that reminded her of her southern roots and huge bamboo stands lining the driveways, as well as the native oaks, poinsettias, hibiscus of every color, heliconias, gingers and an orchid house with more than 200 plants. For Jane it was a time of total freedom to roam for miles on her "*chonguito*" ToTo, named for Dorothy's little dog in the *Wizard of Oz*. A *chonguito* is a small native horse, of no pure breed. ToTo became her best friend, as she was fairly isolated from her regular playmates in San Juan for months at a time. Jane applied all the equestrian knowledge she had learned in her Swiss riding school over the years to ToTo's special care and training. She taught him tricks, such as rearing on command, kneeling and bowing.

Life changed for Jane the next year when she turned twelve and, following family tradition, was packed off to the all-girl Rosemary Hall boarding school in Greenwich Connecticut. The persuasive inducement in Jane's case was that there was a strong riding program at the nearby Round Hill Riding Stables. After enduring the strict academics and the rigors of those bleak New England winters, there were the glorious summers at Barranquitas again where she was reunited with her best friend ToTo and the pleasures of roaming the picturesque Central Mountain Range of Puerto Rico.

Jane's life growing up was diametrically opposed to anything I had ever experienced! She grew up in the life of the Puerto Rican oligarchy: well-traveled, well-educated, with European cultural experiences and championship-level competitive horsemanship. In spite of that, or because of it, our life has blended in the multiple ways afforded by a committed marriage, reflecting love of life and people, faith in God, hard work and a commitment to service. Our time together has been both challenging and rewarding. We continue to this day working together in support of many deserving Puerto Rican and Hispanic causes.

Rosa, my mom, and Rafael, my dad. They were married in 1926.

Me in the first home I remember in Brook Avenue, NY.

My family.

The Korean War on
June 25, 1950.

When I started school at City College New York and later at the RCA Institute.

Publicity for my run as Assemblyman in 1965.

Civil rights activist and "Chicago-7" lawyer William Kunstler addresses the inmates in Attica's Prison Yard. I'm seated under the "22" jersey, with Cong. Herman Badillo, head of Gov. Rockefeller's negotiating group on my right, waiting for my turn to address Puerto Rican and other Hispanic inmates.

Congressman Herman Badillo swearing in officers of the Robert F. Wagner Association in The Bronx, NY, n.d. Present at the ceremony were Robert Garcia, Austin Torres, Carlos Cuevas, Mike Nuñez and Frank Gibbs.

President Jimmy Carter invited me to the White House as a member of the 95th Congress.

In 2016, I received NALEO's President's Award.

Jane and I meeting with Fidel Castro.

Service honoring Bob Garcia's contributions.

Jane and me in Old San Juan, PR.

CHAPTER SEVEN

Of Elections and the New "Hispanic" Census

We have to reach out beyond the obvious to have a full life. For me in politics that meant working with people of all backgrounds, not just the movers and shakers. In Congress, it meant reaching across the aisle. Although I've always been a firm Democrat, I have never forgotten that I made it to the House of Representatives because, in spite of the Democrat machine in the borough that rebuffed me for another, it was my Republican friends in New York who put me on the ballot and gave me the opportunity to win my seat.

The mid-term elections in 1978, less than a year after the special election in which I'd been forced to run as a Republican, reconfirmed my popularity in the South Bronx. I won by a landslide and was returned to Congress, but this time as a Democrat. I'd taught the party organization that had always been part of my life a lesson!

I was already separated from my wife Anita and was living in a small South Bronx apartment; I also had a studio apartment in Washington, DC. Politics would almost totally rule my life as I continued in Congress; the only exception was my kids . . . and later Jane.

It was 1979, and each committee of the new 96th Congress met to organize the subcommittees. We'd been through the exorbitant gas prices and rationing imposed during the Arab Oil Embargo, seen home mortgage interest rates hit 18% and were in the midst of the Iran Hostage Crisis. The federal government needed to control spending, and the committees were ready to cut back in order to economize. Having gotten President Carter to name "Hispanic" as a race for the first time on the 1980 census questionnaire, I asked the "powers that be" not to cut the budget for the census subcommittee. Not only did I want a position on the subcommittee, but I wanted the chairmanship.

Because I was among the very newest Democrats in Congress, I was the last one to be assigned committees. I wasn't really surprised, however, when nobody else wanted to be chair of the census sub-committee; it wasn't "sexy" enough for most representatives. Florida's Bill Lehman, the previous chair, was a wealthy car dealer and wanted to move on to something else, and members are only allowed to have one sub-committee chairmanship. Anyway, I was elected the new chair and I made plans to start hearings immediately.

My newly constituted subcommittee had a $70,000 staff position available—a real plum in 1980 dollars—and at first, I thought it would be a good appointment for one of my trusted New York supporters. But after meeting with Mike Ferrell, who was already in place on the committee and doing an excellent job as staff director, I changed my mind. He greatly impressed me with his competence, hitting the ground running. We put a balanced and effective support staff together. He knew how to pinpoint cities with a lot of uncounted Hispanics and made arrangements to start organizing field hearings almost immediately. Before any important legislation or action comes up in the House, hearings must take place to capture the pulse of the people.

Mike was able to get together all the logistics, people, travel and venues. He was an outstanding organizer and administrator. He acted as sub-committee counsel for the hearings and prepared our questions, while I ran the show as chair. Mike and I worked very hard on the detailed preparations, and I was willing to go all over the country to hold the hearings. It would become a great mission for me, and we finally held about twenty-six hearings in key states with large Hispanic populations, encouraging them to participate in civil government as a key part of the census and citizenship. I'll never forget sitting there at 26 Federal Plaza in downtown New York, near

City Hall, listening to witnesses testify before the committee and my realizing the opportunity and authority I now had to really make a difference for the entire country. It was exhilarating and heady stuff. As a result of the 1980 census, by 1982 the required reapportionment for the growth in the Hispanic population of the United States resulted in double the number of representatives in the House; from five the number had grown to ten! The impact of the Voting Rights Act also was also felt, hundreds more Hispanics were elected all across the country in state and local elections, all the way down to school boards. In a democracy, numbers make all the difference.

One of the new Hispanic congressmen who emerged was a bright and charming Bill Richardson. A Democrat, he'd barely lost a previous election for the House to the Republican incumbent, Manuel Luján. After the census, New Mexico went from two to three representatives, and Bill easily won a new seat, his first elected position, which he went on to hold for fourteen years. He then went on to be elected governor of New Mexico and later be appointed secretary of energy and later still United States ambassador to the United Nations. Bill was Hispanic on his mother's side; she was from Mexico. Bill spoke fluent Spanish. He became a great leader in the Hispanic Caucus, the Democratic Party and in our country overall.

NALEO

In 1976, Los Angeles Congressman Edward Roybal, first elected to Congress in 1963, founded the National Association of Latino Democratic Officials. In 1978, he asked me, Herman Badillo, "Kika" de la Garza and Puerto Rico's Resident Commissioner Jaime Benítez to join him in the formation of a broader, non-partisan, successor organization to be called the National Association of Latino Elected Officials (NALEO). Roybal and his Chief of Staff Harry Pachón were the brains that put this organization together; it still stands today as a beacon of hope and inspiration for many younger and future Hispanic candidates for public office. NALEO's name has been further expanded to include appointed as well as elected Latino officials. According to their own figures, in 1996 there were

3,743 Latino elected officials in the United States; in 2011, 5,850. Following the 2016 general elections, there were 6,100 Hispanic elected officials in the United States . . . quite an accomplishment.

NALEO has proved itself over the years. As the largest minority in the United States, at close to 58 million (including the inhabitants of Puerto Rico), there are many more young Hispanics who will be running for public office in the decades ahead. I was honored to be the recipient of NALEO's President's Award at their 33rd Annual Conference in Washington, DC in 2016.

The Aquinas Senior Housing Project

During the Reagan administration, Saint Aquinas Church in my district asked for my assistance in getting funding for senior citizen housing, which was sorely needed. I called Philip Abrams, the undersecretary for Housing and Urban Development to inquire as to the status of their application, only to be told that the City of New York had failed to complete the necessary paperwork to complete this transaction; the project would not move forward and the project was officially dead. I pleaded with Abrams, but my pleas fell on deaf ears. I then decided to call Max Frankel, who at that time headed the editorial board of the *New York Times*, to see if I could enlist the *Times*' support in getting the Aquinas seniors' project back on track.

He immediately had a reporter assigned to make the necessary inquiries at HUD. Three days later, a story on the Aquinas housing project appeared in the *New York Times*, followed by an editorial a week later concerning the housing situation in the Bronx. The following Monday, I received a call from HUD Secretary Samuel Pierce himself to tell me they had reversed their position and that the Aquinas Housing 202 Project would move forward. To this day, there are more than one hundred units of housing for senior citizens that are used, thanks to Max Frankel and the *New York Times*.

I also remember the day in 1987 when the founders of the Campus Crusade for Christ, Vonette Bright and her husband, called on me as chairman of the committee with jurisdiction over designating Days of Recognition in the United States—the law calling for such days had been signed by President Harry S. Truman in 1952. Vonette was requesting Congress to specifically designate and declare the first Thursday in May as the "National Day of Prayer." There being no such thing as "too much" prayer, no matter what your belief system, I immediately consented and assured her that I would get the bill to the floor of the House as quickly as possible and that I would be honored to be part of that legislation. I did. It was passed and was signed into law in 1988.

NATO

During all this time I was asked by the US delegation to NATO to stay close to Spain, encouraging the Spanish government to formally join NATO; Spain only had observers in the meetings. I was the chair of our NATO delegation and Representative Burton usually wanted me present as an observer whenever we would deal with Spain because I was Hispanic. After a referendum in which the Spanish voted in favor of membership, the country entered NATO. The flag of Spain was added to the others at a ceremony in Brussels in 1982, with President Ronald Reagan and British Prime Minister Margaret Thatcher looking on.

During the Reagan Administration and the deliberations surrounding his proposed "Star Wars" Strategic Defense Initiative, most European countries were against this anti-ballistic missile initiative of the United States. Unusually, the next NATO conference was set for Oslo, Norway. Traditionally, NATO meetings were not held in October because the US delegation's congressional members needed to be attending to campaigns prior to the November elections. But France insisted on holding one in October. As chair of the US delegation and confident of winning the South Bronx again, I could and therefore would represent us in Oslo. But as the only sitting member of the delegation, I had to juggle chairs back and forth, literally running from room to room to different conference meetings.

At one meeting, while I was sitting in a session in another room, the French delegate started pounding away at the United States in the Agricultural Sub-Committee, snidely criticizing our absence for a vote; he stated that it was "yet another snub" from the Americans toward European concerns. Coming from the Bronx, I am no expert on agricultural issues; my constituents had no cows or pigs, fields or crops. My Staff Director Peter Abbruzze quickly but calmly came to find me at the other committee to let me know what was going on. I hurried over there, put on the interpreters' headphones and lashed out at the Frenchman, reminding them all that, contrary to tradition, he had pushed to have the meeting on this date in spite of our objections due to our pending election preparations, and that everyone there well knew that, as a result, I was the only delegate representing the United States. He'd mistakenly thought he could get away with bashing my country when there was no one to respond. I had little problem giving him "tit for tat."

The vote was called, and I ran back to my previous committee.

The NATO committees met twice a year in major cities of the sixteen participating countries (fourteen from Europe and two from North America: Canada and the United States): Munich, San Francisco, London, Lisbon, Rome, Oslo, Paris and so on. The host cities and their countries treated us like royalty on those occasions, and we usually met the kings and queens of the different countries that still had monarchies. It was fascinating and enriching for me and perhaps even more so for my new wife, Jane, who usually went with me, as did most of the congressmen's spouses as participants in cultural exchanges. In addition to having the *savoir faire* that one does not often acquire growing up in the Bronx, and speaking fluent Spanish and French, Jane has natural savvy and was a quick study. She was a terrific asset in that group, easily holding her own with congressmen, foreign delegates and, of course, the wives. Jane studied all the prepared staff material in detail and quickly absorbed every important fact in her "filing-cabinet" memory, making my job so much easier and often much more fun.

Often my work in Congress dealt with international issues, overlapping with some items at NATO in interesting and unexpected ways. A good example was my work on the Civil Service Committee. I was in charge of holiday legislation, important for its symbolism within our communities all over the country. It was especially impactful for a member of Congress to signal this importance through the designation of a special commemorative day, week or month celebrating something special or unique. That had to be done by introducing a bill, a subsequent positive vote in committee and then to the full House for final passage, just like any other piece of legislation.

In 1992, a presidential "Special Commission on the Quincentenary" was formed to commemorate the 500th anniversary of the discovery of America, which had great meaning, especially for Americans of both Italian and Hispanic descent. All of those named to this Special Commission were essentially presidential appointments for an eight-year term. The house speaker and senate president could name two persons each with the remaining members to be directly appointed by President Reagan. One day, Speaker Tip O'Neill called me over to him on the House floor to consult with me about putting Jane on the committee as one of his two nominations. He said, "Garcia," as he usually referred to me in his gruff manner, "all your work on this thing and you cannot serve, but what if I nominated Jane . . . is that okay with you? She can speak the languages, moves like a bullet and has great public relations skills." How could I object? She was a natural. I was delighted, and so was she that evening when I gave her the news.

Jane tackled the commission work with vigor and did her usual thorough preparation. It wasn't long after that when elections for internal committee assignments were held during the first few meetings, and she was nominated and elected chair of the special commission's Internal Foreign Affairs Committee. I will never forget how proud I was when Commission President John Gaudi reported back to me following a heated moment during a meeting that the Nicaraguan delegate to the regional meeting, an "in-your-face" Sandinista, was recognized from the chair to speak; he attacked the commission for holding the meetings in English, when everyone except the United States spoke Spanish, that it was "more authentic" to make Spanish the official language.

Gaudi recounted how Jane's hand had shot up in a flash, and she answered the Nicaraguan delegate (in Spanish first), that with more than 20 million Hispanics (this was in the 1980s) the United States was officially the fifth-largest Spanish-speaking country in the world and that she was sure the United States would find Spanish-speaking delegates to represent them and speak at any future meetings in Spanish . . . if the commission decided to take that route. She added that the world of commerce, finance and politics used English as the official language for those international exchanges and English was taught even in China and Russia, so it seemed to her the Spanish-language idea was rather provincial and totally out of sync with the rest of the world.

When she sat down, there was universal applause, and not another word was said regarding the Nicaraguan delegate's suggestion. Tip O'Neill had been right: she could hold her own. I was damned proud.

As we prepared for the official quincentenary celebrations in 1992, I was on a congressional delegation trip with NATO. During the overseas visit, we took a two-day side trip with a delegation of senators to Madrid, Spain. We were to officially meet with King Juan Carlos at the Moncloa Palace at his personal request. The king had invited us to discuss the role that Spain, an important member of the future Quincentennial Commission, would play in the official celebrations. At that point, we had yet to pass any legislation in the US Congress creating the US Quincentenary Commission, and he was anxious that Spain receive proper recognition. He wanted to know if Spain was seen as a partner or an afterthought, indicating he expected that it would be as a full, participating partner.

During our meeting I addressed him directly in my rather basic Spanish: *Soy Roberto Garcia Rodriguez Gonzalez Roche, representante de la Cámara de Representantes de Estados Unidos. Con un nombre así prometo que España será representado con igualdad en las celebraciones del Quinto Centenario."* (I am Roberto Garcia Rodriguez Gonzalez Roche, a member of the US House of Representatives, and with a name like this I promise that Spain will be equally represented in the Quincentenary celebrations.)

The king was at first surprised that I, a US congressman, was addressing him in Spanish and then pleased with my promise.

The legislation creating the commission, including my promise, was subsequently passed by Congress and became law. To the best of my knowledge, it would be the first time in US history that a foreign country had been included—in this case two: Spain and Italy—as non-voting members of a US presidential commission. We understood just how important it was to the king, and to Spain, to be able to claim a major role in the celebrations to come, since traditionally everything pertaining to Columbus was claimed by the Italians in the United States. But there was a prestige and commercial concern as well: Seville would, at the very least, be co-hosting the 1992 World's Fair with Chicago, which would celebrate the 100th anniversary of its famous Columbian Exposition of 1893, along with the Quincentennial. As it turned out, Seville would go on to host the fair alone, but that's another story, involving Argentina's Falkland Islands and a mini-war with Britain.

Later that same year, the Spanish Institute on Park Avenue in New York City had an official reception for King Juan Carlos and Queen Sofia to commemorate Spain's participation in the commission, and Jane and I were given the opportunity to spend some time with them. As the party was ending, Jane and I departed, following the Spanish monarchs down the institute's winding staircase at a discrete distance. We reached the first floor after they were already out on the street and about to get into their waiting limousine. All of a sudden, the Queen surprised her security detail and all of us by turning around and quickly walking back into the building's entry; everyone thought she'd forgotten something. Apparently, she had. With a gracious, warm, smile she came straight up to me, extended her hand and said, "Thank you, Congressman Garcia, for all your help regarding the Quincentennial!"

Everyone around was amazed, and I was dumbfounded that a queen would go out of her way like that. A Princess of Greece before marrying Juan Carlos, she was a most gracious lady. I don't remember exactly what I said beyond "Thank you," but I do remember thinking, "Wow! Here I am, and my father worked as a laborer at the

Central Aguirre sugar mill in Puerto Rico. Only in America!" I felt deep gratitude that my neighbors in the South Bronx had elected me to the Congress of this great country and had given me this magical moment in my life.

Back to that congressional delegation side trip to Madrid years earlier, we had a very interesting interview with Felipe González, then deputy minority leader of the Spanish legislature (*Las Cortes*). González, representing the part of southern Spain known as Andalusia, was handsome and confident. I knew that he was a man of destiny, despite the four of us being squeezed into what literally had been a broom closet for his office.

I also had taken advantage of going to Spain to arrange a meeting with an important old friend, Jesús Polanco, the founder and owner-publisher of one of the country's newest newspapers, *El País,* founded in 1976, and his editorial staff. Polanco was one of Spain's wealthiest entrepreneurs and a major socialist. His long-time dream of owning a newspaper had materialized and he'd just started up his left-of-center daily, which has gone on to become one of Spain's most influential papers. I had met him well before then, during the Franco regime, as he had been interested in getting involved in educational materials for the Spanish-speaking community in the United States. He had been visiting New York and came to visit me when I was a still a member of the New York State Assembly, which allowed its members to accept jobs and work from outside the legislature.

Polanco greeted me warmly, as we hadn't seen each other in years. As we spoke and I went into detail as to why I was in Spain with an American delegation, he got an idea: Would I be able to arrange a dinner meeting for some of his editorial board and international political writers while we were in Madrid for a few days? He would pull it all together. I agreed to propose this to our delegation's leader, Senator Charles Mathias, and call him the next morning. Mathias agreed and the dinner was on.

After going through what seemed like endless protocol and organizational details and complying with the newspaper's request that this be a meeting attended only by the delegation of senators and congressmen, I got a call from the US Ambassador in Spain, Terrance

Todman, who also wanted to be present. At first, I refused the request outright, thinking we would have a freer discussion with the Spanish press as members of Congress. When I reported the exchange to Senator Mathias however, he explained to me that in his view it would be somewhat of an insult not to honor his request because Ambassador Todman, as our official representative to Spain, would surely be embarrassed to be left out. Frankly, it was a great lesson for me in protocol. I realized that Mathias was right, then called the ambassador back and invited him to join us. All went well.

The meeting was fascinating. The pages of *El País* were rabidly anti-United States, anti-NATO and pro-Felipe González and his Socialist Party. In person, these "Young Turks" on its editorial board were interesting and polite enough; when we met with Jesús and them at Madrid's Palace Hotel, we were also trying to understand the new, post-Franco Spain and absorb the European political currents pulling it this way and that. The streets of Madrid were full of anti-NATO demonstrations.

Anyway, a year or two after our "broom-closet" office meeting, González and his Socialist Party won a major election. And sometime later, since life and politics are that way, the Spanish voters who had elected an anti-NATO socialist government also chose, in a referendum, to enter NATO. Prime Minister Felipe González officially requested it, and Spain was granted membership.

Spain's Recognition of Israel

Several years later, González and I would meet again. I had been elected chair of the new Congressional Hispanic Caucus. I had brought with me a letter addressed to him as the head of government and signed by the few caucus members there were at the time. We were officially requesting the Spanish government to recognize the State of Israel. Spain was the only country in Europe that did not then have diplomatic relations with Israel. I had gotten the idea for this strategy from another political experience. When Ed Koch had first been elected mayor of New York City, President Jimmy Carter came a-calling. I was part of the reception committee at the heliport on what was then the iconic Pan Am Building at the foot of Park Avenue. Mayor Koch took the opportunity, with all the New York and international media present and TV cameras blazing, to publicly present the president a letter signed by all the city's Jewish organizations protesting his treatment of Israel. Talk about putting someone on the spot. Not being as flamboyant as Mayor Koch, I skipped the media part, but took advantage of that auspicious official occasion involving the VIPs of both our countries to present my hand-delivered request to Spain.

It happened like this. When Jane and I arrived at the elegant Spanish consulate, one of the first people who came to greet us was former Governor Luis A. Ferré of Puerto Rico. When he became one of the official members of the Congressional Quincentennial Commission, we sometimes traveled together to Spain and met at many events of the official commemoration. During the course of that evening, Jane and I paid our respects to our host, the Spanish ambassador, and to Prime Minister Felipe González. It seemed an appropriate moment to hand-deliver our official letter of request to the prime minister and to renew our acquaintance. We discussed the contents of the caucus' message requesting that Spain recognize Israel.

Within a few months (the blink of an eye in diplomatic time), I had received an official response from Prime Minister González stating that the government of Spain was working on the issue of recognition of Israel through all the official channels, but as a first step, he wanted me to know that Iberia, Spain's national airline had just signed a pact with the national Israeli airline, El-Al, to begin flights between Madrid and Tel-Aviv. Within a year, Spain and Israel had established formal diplomatic ties.

I was so proud of the results of my initiative as the Congressional Hispanic Caucus leader and realized the potentially important impact our small Congressional Hispanic Caucus could have on the world stage if we recognized the opportunities that presented themselves. The congressmen of Hispanic descent, by working together, could achieve much.

In 1981, I made my first trip to Israel. Menachem Begin, the prime minister, had just been reelected for a second term, and Jane accompanied me on the trip, along with the newly elected senator from Iowa, Chuck Grassley. The day we arrived in Israel was the equivalent to our Inauguration Day, the day Menachem Begin would be forming his new parliamentary government. The Likud party, which he headed, had won by the slimmest majority, so he had no choice but to form a coalition government. Senator Grassley and I were in Begin's office for close to an hour and a half, and at first I could not for the life of me understand why he was giving us so much of his valuable time on such an historic day for the Likud Party. Then it dawned on me: there were leaders of at least ten different smaller political parties waiting outside his office ready to negotiate their roles in his new coalition government. I then realized he was using our presence as an excuse to stall for time because there were so many decisions to be made at that precise moment, and I'm not sure he was prepared to make them.

The Clout of US Hispanics

It was Spain, under the six-year leadership of its brilliant career diplomat in Washington, DC, Ambassador Antonio de Oyarzábal, and his most impressive American wife, Beatrice Cabot Lodge de Oyarzábal, that first realized the importance of the US Hispanic community in the international and national political world. Spain was the first country to reach out to our Congressional Hispanic Caucus Institute's foundation to sponsor educational, trade and cultural ties. This gave us a certain *gravitas* in awakening the sleeping giant of Hispanic political and economic power in the 1980s.

One of the legends in Congress was Representative Claude Pepper of Florida, an extraordinary man who served for forty years in both the Senate and the House of Representatives. As I was the chairman of the subcommittee for the 1980 census, members of Congress would always query me as to how the population for their respective states was shaping up. Every congressman had to know as soon as possible whether his district would remain the same and, if not, how much of a change there could or would be.

Representative Pepper was no different. He was very concerned and he always called on me to find out what the situation looked like for his Miami district. Pepper was in his early eighties, when most folks are no longer buying green bananas. But Pepper was as optimistic as a twenty-year-old regarding his longevity. It was about this time that the Cuban community of Miami and South Florida was starting to flex its political muscle, and Claude knew that his time would soon come to an end. He had been a great representative of the Miami community and especially its elderly, earning him a cover on *Time* magazine as their champion. Claude went on to serve several more terms before his death in 1989. He was replaced by a dynamic young Cuban by the name of Ileana Ros-Lehtinen, a Republican reflecting the state's changing demographics and its right-leaning Cuban population.

Hispanic Heritage Week

Signed into law by President Reagan in 1988, Hispanic Heritage Week was extended to a full month, from September 15, the eve of Mexico's Independence Day, to October 15, just past Columbus Day. Of course, around this time, I used any and all invitations to speak at official events as an opportunity to promote the Spanish participation in the discovery of America, enhancing the image both of Hispanics and of the Congressional Hispanic Caucus. On one such occasion, President Carter's Secretary of Health and Human Services Joseph Califano (of Italian origin and proud of it) invited me to address the Health and Human Services employees at an official gathering.

I just had to get a zinger in about my own Hispanic heritage by remarking that Columbus might have been Genoan and that Italians therefore had a right to be proud of him, but they should never forget that it was a Spanish woman who gave him the money to get here! It got a laugh, and it became one of my standard lines in those early days after the Quincentennial Commission's creation. It was a tremendous time, with a great surge of pride in the United States. And I was so proud to represent the South Bronx and Congress in the celebrations, and to be able to help lead Hispanics at the congressional level.

Puerto Rico Politics and Economics

Once, my father and many islanders had worked in sugar cane, a labor-intensive industry. Extreme poverty had sent them and many others north, and many all the way to Hawaii, to seek jobs. But by the 2000s, the island was a different community from what my parents had known. All kinds of economic experiments and tax incentives had been floated to try to stimulate the respective economies of both the United States and Puerto Rico. We'd even thought of trying the same model as the island's "Operation Bootstrap" for depressed areas in New York. Each decade saw new models, some successful and some not.

Puerto Rico's economy had begun to change from an agricultural economy to a manufacturing one in the World War II years. In this transition, many unskilled laborers and their families had migrated to the United States. Throughout the fifties and sixties, the Popular Democratic Party's social programs helped to improve housing, infrastructure and education, although the economic structure simply could not provide enough jobs. According to economist James Dietz, a welfare-type structure from above had been created, while the means to support it locally had not.

In the 1960s and '70s, the government had searched for many ways to create an economy to sustain its people. One was tax incentives created by Congress and the Puerto Rican government to bring US firms to create factories and jobs. Specific guidelines established that the moneys had to stay in Puerto Rico to bolster the island's economy, which it did for years. It initially worked well. Many US and multi-national firms eventually began operations on the island; initially textile and then pharmaceutical companies moved to Puerto Rico and flourished. At one point, some 50% of the ethical drugs in the world were being manufactured in the island's factories. But as time went on, the capital investment-based (not payroll-based) tax incentives attracted factories with expensive machines installed that required few locals to run them. The goal of creating jobs was eclipsed by a corporate welfare situation that had mainland taxpayers subsidizing the purchase of European production machinery installed in Puerto Rico instead of helping provide jobs for their fellow citizens. President Bill Clinton and Congress later scrapped the program and failed to replace it with a payroll-based tax incentive.

Politically, Puerto Rico's official name of Estado Libre Asociado (strangely but wisely translated as "Commonwealth") was showing its flaws. Congress insisted on keeping its sovereign control over its territory and the Puerto Rican constitution it had approved. Over the years, the movement for Puerto Rico to become a state of the Union grew, but Luis Muñoz Marín, the fashioner of the commonwealth status, opposed statehood, always promoting the status quo. When he died, a giant had fallen.

When I saw no one, not even Puerto Rico's elected representative, the resident commissioner, was moving to present a congressional resolution memorializing Muñoz, I called Tip O'Neill, Speaker of the House, and got his backing to move in that direction. We drafted a bill eulogizing Muñoz Marín, and I then called on the White House to send a representative to Puerto Rico. After several hours, we got President Jimmy Carter to send a member of his own family to the funeral services in San Juan as his representative. As a consequence, we flew down to Puerto Rico on Air Force One.

When the resolution eulogizing Muñoz Marín was introduced, Jack Kemp, whom I'd always distrusted as an arch-conservative Republican congressman from New York, got up and fulsomely praised the Puerto Rican hero. Kemp doing that? What an odd surprise! But beyond whatever feelings he truly may have had for Muñoz Marín's accomplishments, he had another purpose as well. Following approval of the resolution, we talked a bit in the House, and shortly afterwards he called me about his ideas for proposed tax-free "enterprise zones" for distressed urban areas that would take a leaf from Muñoz's "Operation Bootstrap" book in Puerto Rico. We became friends and allies in the cause.

The Enterprise Zone Bill

We were a real "Odd Couple": All-American football player Jack Kemp, a nine-term congressman from the Buffalo, New York, and Nuyorican Robert Garcia, a momentary Republican and two-term (at that point) increasingly vociferous Democrat from the Bronx, co-sponsoring legislation to create "enterprise zones" in the United States.

At a profound level, Kemp saw that economic growth entailed freedom to work, save and invest without government micromanagement. Kemp's vision of "enterprise zones" was to give businesses tax and other incentives to locate in the designated areas in order for them to create jobs for the neighborhood residents. Kemp pushed hard for this and other innovative ideas dealing with poverty during Reagan's first term, but then little would be heard about the idea in Reagan's second term. Kemp saw an opportunity to revive the idea with the election of George H. W. Bush in 1998 and Kemp's subsequent appointment as Secretary of Housing and Urban Development (HUD). Federal spending had been a campaign issue, with Bush's "Read my lips . . . No. New. Taxes." promise. But "compassionate conservative" Kemp, in his first appearance in what was expected to be a high-visibility cabinet post for him, also said he planned to make it known that "you cannot balance the budget on the backs of the poor."

As HUD Secretary, Kemp continued to push hard for enterprise zones, which he now liked to call "empowerment zones," and the Kemp-Garcia Bill would create them. The White House also worked hard to finally pass an urban aid bill in the House, including fifty of Kemp's cherished enterprise zones across the nation. But the effort fell apart in the Senate, which turned the bill into a more ambitious vehicle for higher taxes and more spending. The day after losing the 1992 election to Bill Clinton, Bush vetoed the bill.

Legislation was finally enacted in 1993 and expanded in 1997 by subsequent legislation. In 2000, Congress enacted the New Markets Tax Credit as an additional enterprise zone incentive. Today, Democrats and many Republicans believe that Congress passed Kemp's plan in 1993; it didn't. The Clinton administration kept the idea, but with so many changes; it delivered disappointing results, thus demonstrating that "the enterprise zone idea doesn't work." But Kemp's proposal was drastically different from what was passed and implemented. The two versions had similar names but reflected very different points of view regarding government's role in promoting growth and creating jobs. Kemp's strategy was to open up abandoned areas to all comers, with minimal government direction or intervention. The bill finally signed by Clinton created a bureaucratic maze tilted toward big business that discouraged the potential local entrepreneurs Kemp was trying to help. While it was worth a try in the 1980s, the final 1993 bill was flawed. Further, by 2000 the economy and urban America were changing again, and the Kemp-Garcia experiment yielded only mixed results; "ingenious" entrepreneurs (some would say unscrupulous or worse) exploited loopholes in the laws to reap the benefits without creating the promised jobs.

I, nevertheless, have no regrets. With the South Bronx and urban areas across the country looking like post-WWII Europe, many of Kemp's ideas, such as ownership of public housing and these zones needed to be tried. It was a situation similar to FDR's response to the multitudinous social and economic problems of the Great Depression: try it . . . if it doesn't work, try something else.

The Battle for 936 and Jobs

As I stated above, the US government authorized tax incentives to corporations in Puerto Rico in an effort to industrialize the island's economy. Beginning in 1976, Section 936 of the IRS tax code made this program possible, and the Puerto Rican tax code also empowered US corporations to re-locate to the island and deduct corporate taxes that were distributed as dividends to their parent companies. As a result, the industrial base of the island expanded, with manufacturing in particular flourishing, and of course creating many jobs. However, the tax incentives grew to be unpopular on the continent, seen as a way to avoid taxes and, in 1996, Clinton signed legislation phasing out Section 936 over a ten-year period; the program ended in 2006, with disastrous effects for the Puerto Rican economy and its people.

There was a point in 1996 when I had the CEOs of the three largest pharmaceutical companies all sitting in my Washington, DC office. I had taken up the lead in trying to save Section 936 in order to continue supporting the island's jobs and economy. It was ironic that I, as a New York congressman, had become the point person on legislation so important to Puerto Rico and 3.9 million US citizens who had not elected me to speak for them. But since the island's resident commissioner could not vote in Congress, he had no negotiating power. I went on to cajole 228 members of Congress to sign a letter supporting continuation of Section 936; only 218 were needed to pass the bill. Despite our intense efforts, Newt Gingrich's "Contract with America" and President Clinton's need to reduce spending and increase tax revenue resulted in 936 being seen as "Corporate Welfare"; it was eliminated. As expected, fewer companies brought jobs to the island in the years that followed, and many left when their phase-out ended, taking their jobs with them.

The ultimately unsuccessful fight to save Section 936 tax incentives convinced me that the island's 3.9 million US citizens (in 1996) needed four or five representatives and two senators in Congress to assure its economic stability and success as a society. Those voting representatives and senators from Puerto Rico could have fought for a replacement IRS incentive that was proposed, perhaps a payroll-based Section 30A, more directly tied to job-creation, which was proposed but never passed. How could it have been passed, without Puerto Rico having any vote on the House floor . . . or future votes to trade? Imagine the impact four or five representatives and two senators would have had on the island's present debt crisis and its future going forward, if it had access to the enormous, growing power of Hispanics in government, and tapping into that power . . . simply extraordinary!

CHAPTER EIGHT
Friends and Personages

Phil Burton

My very first mentor in Congress was a great teacher, Phil Burton from San Francisco. As soon as I was elected, he called me in New York City to warmly welcome me and make sure that since I was a registered Democrat (although elected as Republican) I would be caucusing with the House Democratic Caucus, of which he was chairman and a force to contend with. Burton had boundless energy and never stopped working. His political philosophy matched mine on issues of social justice, minority representation and the defense of the working poor. He was an old-time quasi-socialist who never gave up the fight.

Phil was a champion of those causes and fought Republican gerrymandering with such vigor that at his funeral Speaker of the House Tip O'Neill mused as part of his eulogy that Democrats in California could envision him in Heaven reapportioning each congressional district in the state. When asked by fellow members how the apportionment was going in their districts, his favorite expression was, "Don't worry! You're in your mother's arms."

Charlie Rangel

Charlie was one of my favorite people, another boy from a poor area of New York City who went to Congress. He was a hell-raiser, a brilliant man with a lot of heart who helped his district and the city immensely. He saw combat in Korea and came home with a terrible injury but went on to study law and enter politics. Like me, he was an ardent Democrat. He was always an important ally in representing the needy of New York City. He eventually became chairman of the powerful Ways and Means Committee, second only, really, to the speaker of the house.

Mayor David Dinkins

Mayor David Dinkins, my fellow Democrat, was the first black person to be elected Mayor of New York City. Smart and well-educated, reared by his single father in a working-class family, he became a Marine and then a lawyer before entering politics. He'd been my good friend for years, and one of the big disappointments in my political life was that I left Congress just before he was elected mayor in 1991.

We both entered the New York State Assembly in 1965, the first year after the Voting Rights Act was signed by President Johnson with Martin Luther King standing behind him at the White House. As I have stated before, the law opened the door for minorities to be elected to many state and national positions.

When I got to debate my first bill in the Assembly, a piece of legislation that was designed to help the small Hispanic grocery stores, called *bodegas*, I discovered that as a non-lawyer I was not aware of the New York State law pertaining to liquor licensing. It was lawyer Dave who rose to bail me out before I made a complete fool of myself my very first time in debate on the floor. I was very appreciative, and we became fast friends.

There is strength in numbers. Both Blacks and Hispanics were small minorities in the state capitol at Albany. Wanting to band together on issues important to both groups, Dave and I co-founded the legislature's Black and Puerto Rican Caucus in 1966, together with Percy Sutton and Basil Paterson, whose son went on to serve as governor of New York decades later. I was the only Puerto Rican then, but a few others were elected to the Assembly later. The caucus is still going strong, now under the more inclusive name of Black and Latino Caucus, with annual conferences in Albany that attract thousands of Latino activists and politicians from throughout the entire state.

Dave and I, both now retired from elective politics, have remained good friends, still just as committed to civil rights and brotherhood.

Congressman Mo Udall

Maurice Udall, called "Mo" by everyone, was a giant of a man at 6'6" and, not surprisingly, a former professional basketball player. Coming from a family of distinguished public servants in Arizona, Mo was a born leader. He was sharp, but low key—an unusual and fascinating combination in politics.

I'd been a Udall delegate from Manhattan's East Side at the 1976 Democratic Convention at New York's Madison Square Garden when he ran for president. In Washington as a new congressman from New York two years later, I ended up on the Post Office and Civil Service Committee of the House, of which Mo was a senior member. He quickly became my mentor. Known for his self-deprecating wit and quotable comments, he once remarked, "Let's turn inflation over to the post office. That'll slow it down!" But this committee was no joke.

Mo Udall's support had ensured that my amendment to the Civil Service Reform Act, known as the "Garcia Bill," calling for qualified minorities to be actively recruited for Civil Service exams, sailed through. It was voted on and passed by the full Congress. In return, I was later able to help Mo on a piece of legislation especially dear to his heart. His state of Arizona is a desert state with chronic water needs. When major water legislation was being hotly debated in the House, and I saw Mo standing in the Well with a look of anguish at the tied vote, I realized how important it was to him.

I walked over and asked Mo, "Can you use my vote?"

"Yes, Bob," he said.

I'd previously voted "no" with a red card, not on the merits of the bill, but basically going with the flow. After the interchange with Mo, I went up with a green "yes" card and switched my vote for him. Seconds later, the gavel sounded to announce the closing of votes. The bill passed in his favor, by one vote.

That is how Congress works: give and take and personal relationships.

Lindy Boggs

Marie Corinne Boggs, known as "Lindy," was a highly esteemed political figure and a true southern lady in the very best sense of the word. Lindy had married House Majority Leader Hale Boggs, had four children (including two successful politicians and radio journalist Cokie Roberts) and entered politics herself. In her early years, she'd been an English teacher. I'm sure she had been a great one!

Following the death of her husband, she ran and won eight times as the first female representative from Louisiana and made her mark in many ways. In most of those elections, she got more than 80% of the vote, including after her district was redrawn and had a mainly black electorate. She was named permanent chairwoman of the 1976 Democratic presidential convention, the first female to be so honored. In 1997, President Clinton appointed her US ambassador to the Holy See (the Vatican).

She was a highly intelligent woman and a "people-person." When I was first getting to know her, my sister Aimee Cortese had been invited to give the opening prayer for a session of Congress. Aimee was the first woman chaplain of the New York State Prison system and one of the very few women pastors ever invited to give the opening prayer in Congress. Lindy came down to the Well of the House to welcome Aimee; afterwards, she and the few other congresswoman came to meet her at a small reception in my office in the Longworth Building.

Later, we worked together when I was chair of the Census Sub-Committee, which included commemorative legislation, and Lindy came up with the idea of creating a national flower. Many varieties of roses grow in every state. Apparently, Senator Bennett Johnson (D-Louisiana and active in status debates about Puerto Rico) liked the idea too, and had the Senate draft a companion bill, despite Senator Everett Dirksen's longstanding campaign on behalf of the marigold. We drafted the flower legislation in the House together, and Lindy, in her signature red suit, led the bill and got the sponsors and votes.

Whenever I saw Lindy in that red suit, I knew she was in "battle dress" and would not be denied. She'd give me her nicest smile whenever I mentioned her being girded for battle in those red suits. The rose bill also passed in the Senate, and today the rose is our national flower, thanks to Lindy.

One day as we were talking on the floor of the House, I asked Lindy if she could arrange for a group of students from Berger High School in my New York district to meet with a Supreme Court justice during their field trip to the nation's capital. Lindy was a leading spokesperson for the Supreme Court in Congress. She immediately said yes and arranged for my youngsters to meet not with just any of the justices, but with Chief Justice Warren Burger himself. What was supposed to be a ten-minute photo-op turned into a one-hour love-in between these Black and Hispanic young people from the South Bronx and this pillar of a man from Minnesota, who happened to be the chief justice of the United States.

I was truly honored to have her as a friend. She died in 2013 at ninety-seven.

Mother Teresa of Calcutta

Mother Teresa needs no introduction from me. The world is very aware of her leadership and service to the most downtrodden in society: "the least among us." Though she began her cause in India by helping the destitute to die in peace, her order of nuns, the Missionaries of Charity, has spread throughout the world, including six chapters in New York. She won the Nobel Prize for Peace in 1979.

Mother Teresa would come to New York City to visit her nuns and see their work at the Saint Rita Convent in the South Bronx. My office called to see if Jane and I could pay her a courtesy call. It was no small thing, because by then she was frail and in poor health. Just the day before, she'd greeted Princess Diana on the street in front of the convent, hands together in prayer and bowing. Although greatly fatigued, she agreed to see us. As a Catholic and fervent believer in the Church, Jane was ecstatic.

We'd seen her several years before at a National Prayer Breakfast at the Washington Hilton in DC. The ballroom was packed with dignitaries, including President Clinton and his wife Hillary. Each year a prominent person was asked to speak on his spiritual values, and when it came time for her to speak, Mother Teresa came out from the curtains behind the dais and began to speak about the need for love within the family, for one's neighbors and the poor. She really lashed out at the lack of love, about abortion, about dissolution of the family.

The Clintons and Gores on the dais sat stone-faced through it all, but the audience erupted in applause several times. Mother Teresa didn't care that abortion was a hot and divisive political issue and that it is permitted by law in the United States. She was truly special.

So we went to visit Mother Teresa during her visit to the Bronx, that tiny woman dressed in a religious habit that resembled a *sari*, her white robe bordered with blue.

She was unimpressed with my being a congressman and asked, "Just what is it that you do?"

I gave her a short answer and thanked her effusively for working in our neighborhood, which at that time had the dubious distinction of being the poorest congressional district in the entire United States.

Jane's words about this meeting speak from the heart. She remembers that day as one of the highlights of her life. She says, "We entered the room and there was this living legend. I'm short, but I looked down at her . . . she must have been about 4'10" and she was shrunken and bent with age. She looked at me through the most extraordinary eyes I've seen. Penetrating dark eyes, they looked right through me, to my soul. She saw my very mindset and I felt so very flustered. I stammered, but finally got out, 'I am so honored to be in the presence of such a holy saint.' She leaned forward and put her hand on my forearm, replying in a soft but commanding voice, 'My child, we are all called to holiness.' As she spoke, I felt I was outside myself, looking down at us, having an out-of-body experience. It was a transformational moment for me. I was called to be holy! What a perfectly simple, perfect thought! I shall never forget that experience!"

Jane and I will always remember meeting this saintly and outspoken activist, who died later that same year. She is now a saint of the Roman Catholic Church, named Blessed Teresa of Calcutta.

Fidel Castro

We took off in a small private plane from Miami to Cuba, not announcing our plan to the American public. No commercial flights flew that route at the time. Accompanying Jane and me were Congressmen Benjamin Gilman and Hamilton Fish IV, both Republicans of New York, with whom I'd worked in many areas. Jane was our official interpreter on this un-official trip, because Cuba and the United States did not have diplomatic relations, and the public policy of our government was not to negotiate with Cuba. But our mission was to secure Cuban President Fidel Castro's release of four US citizens, all DEA agents, who'd been arrested and imprisoned in Cuba.

In Congress, there has always been a tendency to band together for your state, no matter your party, if you have a good relationship . . . and these two were very good guys. We all got along well. "Ham" was moderate and conciliatory, from a distinguished political family; his father had also been a congressman, noted for being very anti-Franklin Delano Roosevelt. Ham and I had worked together on various projects for New York and he was a good friend. Ben Gilman and I were both elected to the New York State Legislature in 1965 and went on together to Congress. Ben was a leader in many causes, and I always backed him. An accomplished and natural mediator, he'd helped get a Russian dissident out of the USSR during the height of the Cold War. When I was working to free from prison the Puerto Rican nationalists who had attempted to assassinate President Truman at Blair House, he often used to pop into my office to ask, "How's it going?" Even so, he never said what he thought about my efforts.

We landed in Havana and were checked into a what was the big hotel there, I think the old Habana Riviera in pre-Fidel days. It's where they put most official visitors, and I'm sure the rooms were bugged. We were always followed by a group of men and never let out of their sight.

We were shown into Fidel's office late one night; he always had his meetings at night. As usual, Fidel was dressed in his military fatigues and boots and had a big, bushy beard. He was an imposing, strong, prominent figure. He never seemed to smile and seemed to have dictator's manner about him: very much in charge and menacing, with the power of life and death in his hands. Ham and Fidel were both tall, and they looked at each other directly eye to eye.

Castro had studied at the University of Havana Law School, although he always practiced revolution and politics rather than law. He obviously had done his homework; he knew something about each of us.

Jane is petite, about five-one or two. She was the only one of us who was truly fluent in Spanish and she quickly dominated the conversation with Fidel. The other interpreters could not keep up. Of course, Fidel knew English, but refused to speak it with us.

Fidel asked Jane, "*¿Usted es licenciada?*" (Are you a lawyer?)

Jane answered, "*No lo he encontrado necesario.*" (No, I haven't found it necessary.)

Fidel opened his eyes widely and finally smiled at her wise-ass answer. Jane is forceful in character, but charming as well. He obviously liked her.

The meeting lasted a couple of hours. When we finally asked him, through Jane, to free the four Americans who'd been imprisoned, he did not say anything, yea or nay, but just turned around and walked out without so much as a *"buenas noches."* The meeting was over, and we left after midnight.

During the next couple of days, we were bussed around Havana, taken to hospitals and schools, where we were usually offered very good Cuban coffee. Good Cuban coffee was given to VIPs, but most of it was sold, expensively, to Japan rather than to Cuban consumers.

Most impressive, and horrible, was the tour we were given of Combinado del Este, a human warehouse of misery some ten kilometers from Havana. We saw twelve to eighteen men crammed into standing-room-only prison cells. I'll never forget the faces of absolute despair and desperation we saw there that day. It was a real hellhole. And I'd already been in the Attica riot.

Next, we spent a day with some very tough-looking, high-ranking military officers who always had mirrored Ray Ban sunglasses on, even indoors. They took us to another facility and brought out the four DEA Americans and, to our surprise, another American who had defected to Cuba after hijacking a plane to Havana. He wanted to go back to Chicago and his wife and son. He'd been freed after his defection to Cuba, but landed in jail for illegal money laundering, which was considered treason on the island-nation. I think the Cubans wanted to unload him, since he wasn't of any value to them. He eventually was able to strike a deal and returned to the United States, only to serve a term in prison. By comparison, the US prison must have seemed like a luxury hotel.

After a few more days, we were taken to see Fidel, again at night. Our conversation was brief. Once again, he hardly spoke. But this time he asked Jane, *"¿Qué recuerdo quiere llevar usted de Cuba?"* (What souvenir would you like to take from Cuba?)

"Me encantaría llevar café cubano." (I'd love to take back some Cuban coffee.)

Once again, Castro turned and left us without actually answering our petition. However, his aides brought Jane her coffee and gave me a box of top-of-the-line Cohiba cigars, which I later gave to Tip O'Neill, since I didn't smoke cigars.

We left Havana otherwise empty-handed and unsure if we had accomplished anything on the trip. But about a week later, the Americans were released, and we notified the press.

I have no doubt whatsoever that one of the reasons for the mission's success was Jane's having established a rapport with Fidel.

John Cardinal O'Connor, Monsignor Raúl del Valle and Rudy Giuliani

One morning, Jane received a call from her father confessor, Monsignor Raúl del Valle. Cuban-born and reared, he had studied in Rome and gone on to serve many years as pastor of the St. Athanasius Catholic Church that we attended in the South Bronx. A kind and spiritual man, he'd spent much of his time working with the poor and setting up shelters and food stations for the homeless. He'd been Jane's canonical law guide during the annulment of her first marriage and had arranged for our marriage at St. Patrick's Cathedral. He was subsequently named chancellor of the Archdiocese of New York by John Cardinal O'Connor and maintained a close friendship with Jane.

Monsignor del Valle's call was to ask us to breakfast with the cardinal the following week. We happily accepted.

John Cardinal O'Connor was a brilliant and forceful man, son of a union leader and an advocate for the poor, with a PhD in Economics from Georgetown University. Once a US Navy chaplain in Vietnam, he later spoke against nuclear weaponry. We admired his spiritual leadership in the complex and difficult city that was New York in the 1980s and were eager to meet with him.

The following Saturday, Jane and I were at St. Patrick's Rectory promptly at 9:00 a.m. I will always remember the gentleness with which Cardinal O'Connor spoke to Jane and me at that breakfast. Cardinal O'Connor's words of comfort and strength, and the time he spent with us, would fortify us both for what lay ahead. The cardinal prayed with us, blessed us and bid us farewell.

At that time, we were under investigation for allegations connected to the Wedtech company that had been made by the attorney general for the Southern District of New York, Rudy Giuliani. We were not yet under indictment, but it was a frightening time for us both. I was in a state of confusion and sadness, seeing my life so changed by events out of my control. Never before had my personal or public ethics been attacked.

What I think put a target on my back for Giuliani was that a group of politically active people had asked me to consider running for mayor of New York. To that end, focus groups had been organized to identify a minority candidate for mayor and my name was prominent in Democrat circles. I must admit that I was honored by the idea and excited at the possibility of running for the city's highest office. I was tops with registered Democrats in my district. But there was talk that Giuliani was also thinking about running for mayor. Gracie Mansion was not to be in my future.

CHAPTER NINE
Wedtech

The Wedtech corporation and the Small Business Administration (SBA), a federal entity, were giving special loans to minority-owned businesses in the 1980s. Wedtech had been started by a Bronx Puerto Rican, John Mariotta, but one of his partners, Fred Neuberger, quietly acquired more than 50% ownership, suddenly making the company ineligible for the special SBA treatment and millions of dollars in government contracts. However, Wedtech continued to claim it was minority-owned anyway.

An initial federal government investigation mushroomed into something much, much larger because of the shotgun prosecutorial approach that eventually ended up wounding more than twenty people, both in government and in business. In the process of successfully prosecuting the guilty parties, the government (it was later proven) used perjuring witnesses in making its cases. Prosecutorial zeal took on a life of its own, as led by Rudy Giuliani and perhaps his ambition to become mayor of New York, as well as some political opportunism on the part of others.

Jane and I were indicted for extortion and bribery; the indictment had gone forward because of a convoluted mess driven by greed, lies, perjury and criminality. I have to confess to ignorance, stupidity and naiveté on my part. I should have known better; I have no excuse. The multi-layered background of this situation would combine money and politics.

This is what led up to the case. Hundreds of my constituents in the Bronx had been given jobs at Wedtech, Inc., a manufacturer of weapons and other articles for the military, founded by John Mariotta, a reputable entrepreneur in the Bronx. Notable figures such as soon-to-be Senator Elizabeth Dole believed in, and had endorsed, the company. Even the president of the United States had praised Mariotta at the White House. He was a self-made, tool-and-die man who turned a small local business in the South Bronx into a multi-million-dollar corporation fulfilling contracts for the Defense Department. John was a bit inarticulate and lacked real formal education, but he had an understanding of the tool-and-die business. His technical knowledge and enthusiasm made others want to join him and work for him. He also had the vision to understand the potential for turning a quality tool-and-die factory into something really major, while at the same time providing jobs for hundreds of Bronx residents who really needed them. His partner Fred Neuberger had already opened a factory in Israel and was very experienced.

John and I were at a Wedtech-sponsored conference regarding another matter. He put his arm around my shoulder and said, "Congressman, Fred has gotten a factory going in Israel, and I want to do the same in Puerto Rico. Could Jane help Wedtech get a corporation going on the island?"

I answered, "You can't talk to me about that. Talk to her yourself."

So he did.

This exchange was key. He approached Jane. I did not approach him—as simple as that. Jane and an attorney named Ralph Vallone had formed their own corporation to help stimulate business in Puerto Rico; I stayed away from it on purpose for reasons of transparency. They did quite well, including starting up a Benetton franchise in San Juan, something that had grown out of her chance meeting with the head of Benetton Worldwide in a New York City elevator! She was, and is, a bundle of energy and ideas. Whenever she and Vallone had business meetings, I would make a point of being elsewhere, even waiting in an outside room.

My wife's business acumen, connections and vivacity guaranteed her a prominent role in public relations. As many spouses of congressmen have done, and still do, she had opened her own business. Jane had retired from my office staff and had already made her mark in public relations in various areas in addition to Benetton, including Pearl Vision, Revlon and the Spanish International Network (SIN TV which later evolved into Univision). She helped build the nascent Congressional Hispanic Caucus' annual benefit into a major Washington event, and then put together the Hispanic Designers Fashion Show and Benefit for good measure. She was also president of the board at the Bronx Museum of the Arts for five years, where she was again a great innovator.

Wedtech hired Jane and Vallone to help them set-up its Puerto Rico venture. Wedtech seemed like a good client for Jane and Vallone. Even Elizabeth Dole, the future senator, had interceded on Wedtech's behalf in connection with a $32 million contract to produce small engines for the US Army. President Reagan continued to praise Wedtech for bringing jobs to the unemployed. In other words, it was a well-regarded company, not just in the Bronx, but at important levels of government as well.

Specifically, Vallone and Jane had been hired to represent Wedtech in seeking government support in granting the IRS Section 936 status and tax-exemption for a proposed dry-dock and factory in the island, for which fees were charged, a normal occurrence in any jurisdiction's or nation's industrial development procedures. Wedtech was in competition for this contract with the Puerto Rico government, which was always aggressively seeking to attract job-creating investment to the island.

How I became unknowingly involved in this mess was that I made the mistake of accompanying Jane to a dinner with the Wedtech partners in New York one evening. Mario Moreno, who turned out to be a real piece-of-work, was the company's executive director. He had invited her to a business dinner at a great Italian restaurant in Manhattan, Lello. During the trial he testified, lying under oath, that extortion and bribery had taken place at that dinner. No such thing happened. But I was there because there was no way I wanted Jane going out to late dinners with other men—my Hispanic macho-mind—and then coming from Manhattan back to the

South Bronx, where we lived. And, I must admit, I love great Italian food! I had no idea what would be discussed but went along.

And Jane made a mistake, too. She accepted a piece of jewelry, a gift from Mrs. Mariotta, who had become a good friend, and Jane didn't check it out with the Congressional Ethics Office. I told her to return it, but before she could, it was stolen, along with all her jewelry, from our bag at the airport, for which we filed a police report.

When the indictment was eventually handed down, I made a statement to the press, including the following:

> I note that despite an investigation which has lasted nearly two years and has scrutinized virtually every facet of my personal and professional life, the charges deal only with the preposterous allegations of Mario Mareno, one of the most notorious felons of the 20th century. My brush with the criminal justice system has left me deeply shaken as I observed the government harass and intimidate my staff, colleagues, friends and family to induce them to say something negative about me, while virtually ignoring polygraph evidence demonstrating my innocence and all other exculpatory information and testimony. I maintain my innocence and that of my wife and pledge to fight this case with all of my God-given strength.

Giuliani's case was built on those two things, bribery and extortion, and we were indicted and found guilty! The other thing the prosecutors made a big deal about was that I was always having budget problems. A-ha! Motive! After the trial, one of the jurors later said, "We found them guilty because we thought they needed the money."

This point bears clarification. It's fair to say that from my first days as an elected official, I was often overdrawn in my personal finances. It is very costly to be a representative of the people; I was always expected to pick up the tab for a meal, a drink, even a hot dog. Constituents always expected it, especially in poor districts. Therefore, I occasionally was overdrawn, surviving only on my salary and Jane's income. Not surprisingly, many in Congress had and today have the same problem. In fact, years later the House of Representatives Bank reported many congressmen overdrawn at the House Bank, something I never did, because I considered that to be unethical. I considered the House Bank untouchable.

The indictment charged Jane and me with a bribery-extortion scheme, and we went through two trials. Giuliani's prosecutors got two convictions, which, of course, got extensive media coverage. Eventually both convictions would be overturned unanimously on appeal; those did not get extensive media coverage.

As part of the prosecution's case, Mario Moreno lied and wrongly implicated several people, including Jane and me, as having accepted bribes and engaging in extortion. Moreno was sentenced to just two years in jail for his part in Wedtech's crimes. It was a reduced sentence for "cooperating" with the prosecution and testifying against us. Eventually some twenty state, local and federal government officials were convicted, although some were reversed on appeal when it was found that former Wedtech president Anthony Guariglia, a star witness for the prosecution, had committed perjury, and that the prosecutors had known this.

I had declined to testify in my own trial, being intimidated by the whole process. Now I look back and could kick myself for that lack of courage. Where was the lion inside me when it came to defending myself? Was it only there when I defended others against injustice, as I had done often during twenty-five years of public service? It was a jury trial, and I should have been brave enough to trust the people, to step up and speak.

After the guilty verdict, I had had the option of beginning to serve my sentence immediately or to wait until all the appeals had run their course. I chose to begin immediately and put it all behind me as soon as possible, while Jane continued to work with the attorneys on the appeal and collect the hundreds of letters attesting to my character, record of integrity and honesty. At sentencing, I asked to be sent to Florida, because Jane's mother was there.

The sentencing judge said to me, "Mr. Garcia, I suggest you get this behind you and come back. Keep on doing the good work you've been doing for the community all your life."

Those words touched me. I'll never forget them.

Before we could get to the second trial, my attorney, Bob Morvillo, took my case to the US Supreme Court, arguing that I could not be tried under the double jeopardy clause. The Supreme Court, however, refused to take the case. We were then forced to go for a second trial, which would take place in 1991.

In the meantime, I began my sentence at the Elgin Air Force Base compound in the Florida Panhandle. On March 21, 1990, I walked through the gates of the minimum-security prison dressed in civilian clothes, in deference to the fact that I went in voluntarily to get it over with, instead of waiting for the appeals court verdict. Originally built to house 600 prisoners, at that time it held about 1,000 white-collar criminals, including several of the Watergate figures. Not your typical federal prison, and certainly not Attica, it was the first "cushy" facility to be called "Club Fed"—a take-off on the Club Med Resorts then popular.

Nevertheless, I was deprived of my liberty and told what to do and when to do it, kind of like the Army. Starting my term there was the worst day of my life, worse than facing combat in Korea. I had to show an expressionless face to the world and I had to be strong. After all, I was a tough kid from the South Bronx and I could take it. The only good thing I could think of was that my wife's granddaughter, Katherine, had been born just hours before my internment. The emergence of new life would give Jane consolation while she worked with our lawyers on our appeal. I, in turn, would try to use the time to refresh my spirit and mind. Jane would be staying with her mother in Stuart, Florida, and make the five-hour drive to visit me every other week.

I'd reached the pinnacle of my career as a US congressman representing the South Bronx and had shared the stage with national and world leaders. On some twenty-five different occasions, my brethren from the South Bronx had gone to the ballot box to choose me as their leader, first in the New York State Legislature, then in the US Congress. My family was highly respected for its Evangelical Christian leadership in New York, and my father was pastor of the Thessalonica Christian Church. My father's favorite expression, *"su servidor"* (your servant) was branded into my mind, and in fact I associated it with my own lifelong dedication to public service. He was a loving father and husband, and my parents had renewed their vows after fifty years of marriage in that church. He had gone to meet the Lord two years later. My mentor, internationally known preacher Sister Aimee, was the founder and pastor of the vibrant Crossroads Tabernacle, also in the Bronx, where I'd served as deacon.

During the trial, I had thought back to the time my father had come to see me before a judge and how I'd felt that I had let him down and disgraced the family. What would my grandchildren and great-grandchildren think of me? Would they only see the headlines from *The New York Times* stating that their grandfather had gone to prison, and then would they drop their heads and turn away in embarrassment? Would they ever know the full story?

The overturning of my conviction would emblazon newspaper front pages again, just as the lower court sentencing had, but certainly not as prominently as the indictment or conviction. And who reads all the papers all the time? This is one of the main reasons for telling my story in this book. I want my family to know what really happened and to be very aware of the fact that I never lost my integrity. Dedication to public service? Yes. Passion for the Congressional Hispanic Caucus? Yes. Mistakes? Yes. Bad judgment? In this case, yes. Crime? Never.

Obviously, the Appeals Court agreed and overturned the conviction, and the Supreme Court in another appeals case also found in my favor.

Hindsight is 20/20. I'd resigned my seat after the initial trial and threw myself on the mercy of the judge. If, before resigning, I had only waited for the appeals court decision, which turned out to be unanimous in my favor, I would probably have been able to stay in office and even be reelected. And I probably would have been there for a long time. But if you're convicted and remain in Congress, you can't vote on legislation before the House. Some congressmen who have been convicted have done that, stayed put while awaiting the appeals verdict. If I'd stayed in office, awaiting the appellate court's review and ruling, I would have left the people of the South Bronx without a voice. I just couldn't see myself doing that to my constituents.

As it turns out, ironically, there was no major legislation affecting my district during those four months. In other words, if I'd stayed in office while waiting out those four months at Eglin, nothing negative would have happened to my district. Actually, a couple of Republican congressmen asked me not to resign, assuring me that they would hold off on the Ethics Committee's review of the case until my appeals process was finished. Those were the days when parties still talked to each other. But I'd made that decision, and life went on.

I resigned from Congress, knowing that a fellow New York Puerto Rican, José E. Serrano, would take my place. Born in Mayagüez, he grew up in the Millwood Housing projects in the South Bronx and served in the US Army Medical Corps before turning to politics. His son, José Marco, now holds my old seat in the New York Senate, by the way. I consider his father an outstanding person, smart and capable. Over the years we have supported each other, even if the party sometimes disagreed with our decisions. When he first ran for the State Assembly, I was among the first to support him and have never been sorry. He has been an excellent congressman, a great spokesman for his constituents and even for the Puerto Ricans on the island.

It is what it is.

* * *

Upon entering prison, I had no way of knowing what the appeals court would decide. Prison was my reality and would be part of my obituary. Yet my spirit remained unbowed. In spite of prison and having my family battered and career devastated, I felt an inexplicable sense of freedom. It was strange: deep down I wasn't fearful at all—kind of like when the Puerto Rican inmates had surrounded me to protect me inside the Attica riot. I was determined to overcome whatever life would hurl at me. I somehow knew that God would turn all this negativity into something positive. What exactly, I didn't know, but I knew I'd survive . . . and even grow.

How strange life is, so filled with both hope and anxiety at the same time! I'd always been a believer in God, even though I was just a normal man, imperfect and fallen in different ways. I'd known the exciting life of what's called a "mover and shaker," been considered a VIP in the Bronx, where everyone knew me and looked up to me. I'd met alone and even dined with our president in the White House, met the King and Queen of Spain, talked with the generals of China as an envoy of my country, enjoyed my wife trading Spanish ripostes in the middle of the night with Fidel Castro, spoke with the incredible Mother Teresa when she came to the South Bronx, proudly traveled the world as a powerful man, a congressman of the United States of America. I had helped to give form and structure to the aspirations of Hispanics all over the United States. But more importantly, I had had the honor of representing my beloved South Bronx.

Now this experience would offer me a chance to learn the power of rebirth and renewal, to bare my soul to my own self, shake off any remaining hubris and start over. That's how it was as I entered prison, holding on to my faith and, oddly enough, with my heart at peace in spiritual terms. I treasured the good I'd done, the counsel of my sister and the love and loyalty of my wife.

Soon enough, I went into what can only be described as "pastor mode," leading a Bible Study class and helping inmates study for their high school GED exam. Many of the men were having family problems, including receiving "Dear John" letters from their wives and hearing of other painful situations back home. We talked together and I tried to counsel them, give them hope in both practical and spiritual ways. My fellow inmates were bankers, lawyers, drug dealers, embezzlers and others. As far as I knew, none were violent offenders. I'm sure some, like me, were not guilty, too.

In some rather funny ways, it wasn't so very bad. Sharing barracks is like being in the Army, and I'd done that. The good chow — white rice and black beans were the Sunday staple — was prepared by a Cuban cook who was another prisoner. I exercised and played baseball when allowed. I was a pitcher for the over-fifty team. I read a lot. I prayed and thought and worked and hoped Jane would be successful in fighting for our vindication.

I had no way of knowing if the appeals court would reverse our convictions. It didn't help that my attorney, the late Bob Morvillo, didn't encourage me. He said that the New York Circuit Court was conservative and didn't often rule in favor of an appeal. Would my name and reputation and Jane's ever be cleared? Why and how had all this happened, and what would happen next?

Four months after entering, I was back in free society after the appeals court unanimously threw out the finding of guilt. I was free, but without a house, savings or a job. *Nada*. We'd spent everything to pay for our legal representation and appeals.

Jane and I took shelter, first at her mother's house in Florida, for which we were very grateful, but then I had to find a way to make a living. Shortly after our successful appeal, I was asked to run again for Congress. Many of my friends encouraged me to run, counting on popular support from the Bronx because they believed that the voters would consider me a target of persecution as well as having had a sterling record as their political leader. However, I knew José E. Serrano was a good man and that he would continue doing a good job. If it had been anyone else, I would have probably re-entered the arena. But content that my constituents would be well served, I decided my path would lead elsewhere.

Chuck Colson, an extraordinary leader in prison rehabilitation and an inspiring Christian who affected very many lives, would reach out his hand and give me support to go forward in the wake of my personal disaster. I owe him greatly. President Nixon's special counsel, he served time in prison for his part in the Watergate scandal. This brilliant man, tough Marine and hard-nosed lawyer, or "ruthless" as he called himself, had undergone a spiritual awakening shortly before going to prison. It was authentic, not a media event, as some claimed. At Colson's death in April of 2012, *Washington Post* columnist Michael Gerson referred to Colson as one of the most influential social reformers of the twentieth century. Colson had established Prison Fellowship Ministries, a compassionate worldwide ecumenical outreach to prisoners and their families. Gerson stated that Colson's "vast, humane contribution is the best evidence of a faith that is more than crutch, opiate or self-help program. It is the hallmark of authentic religion."

Mulling over those times and the whole subject of prison reform and rehabilitation, I must say that Chuck Colson's spiritual thought, as well as his work on prison reform and rehabilitation, inspired me. He became my dear friend, a man of great faith, zeal, honesty and leadership; I truly admired him. When I left prison, destitute and career-shattered, it was Chuck Colson who offered me a job and spiritual comfort with his Prison Fellowship Ministries. The ministries gave me the incentive to start again.

My wife and I were able to begin to rebuild our lives together and re-forge the bonds of our marriage. We had been exonerated by the law, but this whole process took seven years of my life from beginning to end. Although they had been seven very valuable years of learning and growth, in the end I knew the fear of re-entering the world and trying to earn a living. And as what? A life-long politician, now exonerated but still disgraced, didn't have the brightest future. Who would ever hire me?

Chuck Colson gave me my first job after leaving Eglin. During the months that followed, I was able to re-focus my life and count my blessings. My work with Colson's Prison Fellowship Ministries proved to me that I still had worth. While I was still in prison, Jane had spoken to Tom Barrett, the spiritual leader of the Member's Bible Study group, about the usual preparation for the formality of going before the parole board and the need for support from friends. Many of my Christian former colleagues from Congress wrote letters on my behalf and several came to see me at Eglin. My sister Aimee prayed for me, and when I emerged, counseled me just as she'd done when I was young.

Jane and I came to realize that God had a purpose for us. First, we had drawn closer to God and to each other as a result of this searing experience; we learned to live a day at a time. The experience had stoked a hunger for His Word, satiated in reading the Bible and in our daily devotionals each morning. We shared our faith both in Jane's Catholic Mass and in my Evangelical service. Faith, family and friends have allowed us to recover our broken spirits, mend and go forward.

Looking back, my "prison conversion" was in fact an extension of something that had always been part of my life, beginning as a child in my father's church and even during my years in Congress. For more than twenty years since arriving in Congress I had attended the 8 a.m. Thursday morning Congressional Prayer Breakfast, a bipartisan breakfast—we were always alternating its chairperson: a Democrat one year and a Republican the following year. In the many years I'd attended, I'd listened to the spiritual thought and testimony of many members of Congress. The breakfasts were a place where members with deep-rooted problems poured their hearts out, and never once did I ever hear or read about it in any media outlet. Truly amazing!

I loved the Congressional Prayer Breakfast, because it was truly free of politics. As one of my colleagues in Congress would put it, "It was the best hour of the week." As with most of us when we attend church, we always seem to sit in the same spot every Sunday. Well, the prayer breakfast is no different. Somehow, I always ended up sitting just across the table from Congressmen Wes Watkins of Oklahoma and Charles Stanhom of Texas, invariably talking about their weekend plans. I'd find myself thinking, "What a country we have, where I have two people sitting in front of me talking about what they're going to do this weekend: one is gonna put up fencing for his cattle and the other is gonna look over his crops." I'd find myself marveling at the diversity of the United States and thinking, "What a great country it is! I have a cattleman and a farmer as fellow members of the United States Congress . . . and I represent an urban district in New York City. It would take them hours to drive through their districts, and it would probably take me fifteen minutes without traffic to cross my entire district both north to south and east to west."

In the 1980s this worked for Congress. We truly got along. I sure wish it was the same today. With Congress so terribly divided, it makes it almost impossible to legislate anything.

CHAPTER TEN
Puerto Rico

As an elected official representing my New York constituents, I was careful to not take sides in Puerto Rican politics, which is why I was able to work with all parties to improve conditions for those living on the island. In Congress I became "Mr. Puerto Rico," as I was lobbied intensely by all kinds of island groups: historic preservation groups, the Chamber of Commerce, insurance brokers associations, the Manufacturers' Association and so on, all seeking support for bills in Congress involving banking, fair housing, land preservation, federal benefits, anything that would affect them on the island. When it came to federal legislation, Puerto Rico was usually what I saw as "an afterthought to an afterthought." So whenever possible and beneficial, I would write a codicil or specific language into a piece of legislation, also applying it to Puerto Rico. When it came to the actual conditions on the island, I only knew what I was told by my constituents and by those of the Popular Democratic Party who came up to help during campaigns. But I really didn't know the island or its true problems well. That only comes from being there, from living there.

I had made my very first visit to Puerto Rico in 1953, after being discharged from the Army. When first elected to public office in 1965, I began visiting the island about twice a year. Once elected to Congress, I'd travel there about three times a year for official or politics-related business. I seldom left the capital city of San Juan, and then only to visit family: Estefania, my mother's sister in La Playa de Ponce and my parents in suburban Bayamón. If I was going to Ponce, I'd catch a "*público*," or jitney cab, in Old San Juan, where dozens of them would be waiting to take fares all over the island. "*Cabe uno, ¡cabe uno a Ponce!*" (Room for one to Ponce!) they'd yell. I'd keep quiet and linger until the car was just about full, hoping I could get a discount so that the driver would be able to leave on time.

Those jitney trips were before superhighways or expressways crisscrossed the island. The jitney drive from San Juan to Ponce (only 35 miles "as the crow flies") was three and a half hours of frightening curves and hairpins, drivers tapping or holding down their horns most of the way, snaking up and down the mountain terrain. It was very rural; sometimes on the return trip to San Juan, live animals would join us as passengers—mostly chickens, but also the occasional goat and once even a pig! The noise, the swaying and the smells were enough to daunt most travelers, but after surviving Army life, I braved it. Breakdowns were common, and a stranded passenger would just pack in with the next *público*. Rental cars hadn't made their appearance yet, and I had little money for one anyway.

These memories came flooding back to me recently. In 2013, my wife Jane and I moved to Puerto Rico for my health, and it was my first time living on the island: I love it!

Today's street sounds are different, more electronic and mainly connected to politics and *salsa* and *reggaetón* music as well as traffic noise. We now have supermarkets, Walmarts and Costcos, local markets and even a few organic farmers' markets. We have mass transit in San Juan with the new 17-mile *tren urbano*, air-conditioned buses and fleets of taxis (now joined by Uber drivers as well) that roam the tourist zones or come on call.

Now, with more leisure time, we've ventured out onto the rest of the island, discovering its dramatic beauty and, in some cases, the old way of doing things in *el campo* (the countryside). The names of the towns we've visited all around the island since living here are magical, a mix of Spanish and the native Taíno and Arawak languages: Guayama, Salinas, Patillas, Maunabo, Cayey, Caguas, Ponce, Guánica, Jájome, Rincón, Guajataca, Mayagüez, Sabana Grande,

Arecibo and Dorado. Believe it or not, the mountainous terrain and the resulting difficulty of communications and transportation in centuries past gave birth to seventy-eight cities and towns, each with its own municipal government for a population of about 3.5 million today, down from 3.9 million in 2000.

The true beauty of Puerto Rico is out on the island, outside of San Juan. I could kick myself for having put off experiencing it until now! Time marched on when I was in public service, but we're making up for it now. It has been a great lesson in my own family heritage, for the first time understanding what my father and mother gave me. Both were born in rural Puerto Rico in the early twentieth century, just a few years after Spain had ceded the island to the United States in 1898. I see my father in the south coast landscape of Coamo, Guayama, Salinas, Santa Isabel and the Central Aguirre sugar mill, where he toiled as a machine operator before leaving for New York in 1924 and where he bought milk with company-issued tokens at the company store. I see my mother's sister's house still standing in La Playa de Ponce with a new coat of paint and a new family with children. I see traces of Spanish architecture in everyday homes and fabulous art deco buildings of a different era. All of this is becoming part of me now, too.

Education on the Island

Since moving to Puerto Rico, I've been travelling to the island's schools to encourage young people to go on with their education and to tell them about possible college help through the Congressional Hispanic Caucus Institute and its outreach programs. Changes in education on the island have occurred since my parents' time, but not all for the better.

It has struck me as ironic that despite the arrival of cable tv and the internet in Puerto Rico over the past twenty years, many feel that those who went to school on the island in the first four decades of the United States presence spoke better English than those graduating today—of course, the government did impose English in education during those years. Since moving here, I am stunned by how few of today's public-school graduates speak English well. Unless they've lived and worked in the continental United States during their formative years, they basically don't, or won't, speak even basic English. I'm talking about clerks in Walgreen's pharmacies, supermarket cashiers and government employees. To pay a fine or challenge a traffic ticket, you'd better bring a translator with you, even though both English and Spanish are supposedly official languages for government purposes! There's a huge difference between the island's public schools, which teach all their classes in Spanish and just teach English as a second language, and the many private and parochial schools, which do teach English and Spanish in a balanced way, with excellent results.

Why aren't more of Puerto Rico's people bilingual? Because the speaking of English was increasingly used as a political issue. Control of the island's public education system passed to local governments with the 1952 Constitution and the new Puerto Rican Department of Education quickly becoming the biggest employer on the island with the biggest budget, including ever-increasing federal educational program funds. English ceased to be the language of instruction and was instead taught as a second language in public schools. Worst of all, its use in daily life was officially and unofficially discouraged, especially for the lower classes. Since the 1950s, language was seemingly turned into a political issue. The anti-statehood pressure was so strong that one PDP governor in the late 1980s felt he had no choice but to sign legislation removing English as a co-equal language of government as provided in Puerto Rico's 1952 Constitution. His pro-statehood successor quickly had the legislature repeal that law.

I'm told that in the early 1980s, the island's only English-language daily newspaper, Scripps-Howard's Pulitzer-winning *San Juan Star*, had found it necessary to defend its own existence with an ad campaign insisting that "Being Puerto Rican is not a question of language." The very politicians who pushed for, or allowed, the removal of English as an official language and downplayed its importance in the public schools all spoke English; they had attended US and European universities, and their children had learned the history of Puerto Rico in English in private schools. But they hypo-critically told the poor that speaking English was being a *vende-patria*, or an unpatriotic "sell-out."

The ability to speak fluent English is not about ideology or Anglo superiority; it's about giving the children of Puerto Rico the tools they will need to reach their God-given potential. In my work with NATO, I was always impressed with the English spoken by the young people in many European countries; they seemed to have no identity crisis or complex as a result of being bilingual or multi-lingual. They certainly weren't considered "sell-outs." National boundaries in Europe are so close, they're like the states on the mainland; children easily pick up two, three or even four languages before they even get to high school. Yet the Department of Education in Puerto Rico maintained that the island's children had to learn Spanish well before they could learn English. They maintained that teaching them both languages would be — Can you believe this? — confusing. Were these bureaucrats saying that Puerto Rican children did not have the same innate ability to learn two or three languages that European children have? Rubbish.

Some people are afraid that a bilingual Puerto Rican society would give up its *idiosincrasia,* that is its identity and culture, and become "Americanized." But every country has its idiosyncrasies . . . not just Puerto Rico. As one who is bilingual and grew up bilingual, I can speak of the modest difficulties it posed in my own back-ground. Our parents spoke to us in Spanish, but our outside home environment was all in English. When my own boys were young, we all spoke English at home and consequently they never really learned good Spanish, even though they studied it in school (as have millions and millions of kids). But again, if you don't use what you've learned, you lose it. Although I understood Spanish some-what because of my parents, I found it necessary as a congressman in the early 1980s to attend the Spanish-language classes offered by the US Department of State so I would be able to better conduct offi-cial business in Puerto Rico and explain myself to my constituents directly or in New York's extensive Spanish-language media. I want-ed to be truly bilingual.

To survive its current crisis, Puerto Rico needs to do many things; becoming totally bilingual is near the top of that list. The larger world out there speaks English: international trade, banking, business, politics and diplomacy, law, science, art and music. If Puerto Rico is to benefit from being under the American flag, it should be as it was originally intended after 1898: able to operate in both languages. As it is now, only students whose families can afford for them to go to private schools get a good grounding in English and become bilingual, while the poor are permanently hobbled by only being able to speak Spanish. This only serves to widen the gap between the haves and the have-nots on the island.

Tribal Politics

Puerto Rico is one of the most beautiful places on Earth. Its people are open, generous, upbeat and friendly. Some independent surveys have even proclaimed its people "the world's happiest." The island is sports-crazy and has seen dozens of its ballplayers make it to the major leagues and many of its boxers win world championships. But with an estimated 30% of those who work employed by some government entity, the island's national sport is neither baseball nor boxing; it's tribal politics. "My tribe is better than yours."

Even young children parrot the political opinions they hear at home, or from their teachers and peers at school, with conviction and pride. Because of my electoral experience, I have been asked on many occasions by the Organization of American States (OAS) in Washington, DC to monitor the presidential elections or important referenda in various Central and South American countries. The disappointing and disquieting thread of similarity between their elections and Puerto Rico's is the total lack of a properly conceived and administered, permanent system of civil service to run their governments efficiently and professionally. The unfortunate attitude that permeates the tribal politics both on the island and in these countries is: "*Quítate tú pa' ponerme yo*" (You get out so I can get in)—It's our turn.

There are other factors, of course. The continental United States is all about virtually limitless opportunity and options; if you're not doing well where you are, there's always "greener pastures" out there on the interstate. You can assist and rejoice in a friend's success without envying him. But islands like Puerto Rico and poorer countries can be different. The opportunities are not limitless; the "pie" is perceived as being only so big. If someone else is successful, a stagnant economy necessarily means there's simply less for you. Therefore, you envy another's success, and staying employed is a major source of stress. If you, or someone in your immediate or extended family, work for the government, you probably owe your job to the party. Without civil service, if your party loses, there goes that job and your family's stability.

Beyond democratic and civic motivations, having someone in your immediate family working for the government somehow also helps to explain the average 87% voter-participation rate on election day in Puerto Rico. Election Day there is a holiday from most work and school. But while local politics may be a source of entertainment, the lack of consistent good governance is a source of frustration for all, rich and poor, young and old.

This patronage model gives rise to huge government payrolls; as much as 40% of the population works for the government in some of these countries' patronage systems. This, in turn, develops and maintains a convenient political base. In the thirty-eight years of Muñoz Marín's one-party rule by his PDP, there was an illusion of having a civil service, only because there was virtually no turnover to another party or tribe.

Public service is about dignity and having pride in working toward the solution of your society's many problems. Citizenship is about voting for the best person, not voting to keep a family member's patronage job. Each agency should be required to publish a comprehensive list of requirements for each position, not just those of a government agency's top management. There would, of course, still be a limited need for agency head appointments or *puestos de confianza*.

As part of the solution, I believe the island's universities should develop courses in public administration and management, public policy and leadership, as parts of a civil service curriculum leading to a degree. The University of Puerto Rico already has a similar graduate degree, but undergraduate degrees should be offered as well by it and the island's other universities. Civics in high school, including an exam, should be required for graduation. Conscientious good governance is the key, and young people must get the consistent message that public service is about giving, not getting.

Until some fearless public officials are willing to become true public servants for the good of the whole and lead the charge for change, the island will continue to go from crisis to crisis; trying to patch up what we've got leaves a lot to be desired.

The private sector needs to play its part as well. There has never been the equivalent of an effective "Better Government Association" on the island to serve as a brake on government when it ignores the law or the US or Puerto Rican constitutions. When a governor, for example, has ignored existing law or a constitutional provision, there is no group to publicly and indignantly go to court to seek a Temporary Restraining Order or an injunction against whatever illegal thing the governor or an agency head is trying to do. The private sector needs to hold government accountable.

Puerto Rican Media

During better economic times, Puerto Rico was one of the largest media markets in the world. I'd heard some experts say that only Brazil saw more spent *per capita* on advertising than Puerto Rico. Ad agencies abounded. Talk radio is hours and hours of talking heads giving their opinions as absolute truth. The populace is used to the media telling them what to buy . . . and think.

As in most markets, the circulation and influence of the legacy daily newspapers on the island has been waning for years. Several giants have disappeared, including *El Mundo* (The World), *El Reportero* (The Reporter) and even the Pulitzer Prize-winning *San Juan Star*—a shadow of that daily is still being published under different ownership and under the title *San Juan Daily Star*. For decades, the largest circulation daily had been *El Nuevo Día* (The New Day) when its owner, industrialist and pro-statehood party founder Luis A. Ferré sold the paper to his son on becoming governor in 1968; his son moved the paper to San Juan in 1970 and, over time, the editorial stance of the paper became less pro-statehood and more status-quo.

El Vocero, previously known for its red headlines and *Enquirer*-style emphasis on crime and scandal, was sold out of bankruptcy in 2013 and reappeared as a more mainstream, rather pro-statehood, free-distribution daily; it was the first major daily on the island to adopt that model. Today, its audited circulation during the week is higher than *El Nuevo Día*'s. In 2008, *El Vocero* was joined by a second free-distribution daily, *Metro*, part of the world's largest chain of dailies; audits show that it too has surpassed *El Nuevo Día*, which continues to charge for single-copy sales. Swedish-owned *Metro* touts its being politically neutral, *sin colores* (without colors), referring to the PDP's red, the PNP's blue, the Independence Party's green, etc.

Puerto Rico's TV stations, once producers and exporters of programs, have shrunk to local outlets for the stateside giants of Hispanic TV: Mexican-dominated Telemundo and Univision. Even island television pioneer WAPA is nowhere near the powerhouse it was in the second half of the last century, although it has realized the importance of the Puerto Rican diaspora niche and filled it with a satellite/cable/internet station, WAPA America. The local government's TV channel WIPR, which years ago stopped broadcasting English lessons in addition to the usual cultural and history programming, became increasingly politicized as well. Under the status-quo Alejandro García Padilla administration, the only English-language programs allowed to be broadcast on the publicly supported University of Puerto radio station were classical music programs.

And what is it that is broadcast on television? Every night, it seems, the evening news programs feature (and often lead with) the close-up of a crying woman, the victim of domestic violence. After the segment, the news directors have their anchors, usually a female, look forlornly into the camera and do a *"tsk, tsk, qué terrible . . . hay que hacer algo."* (How terrible; something must be done.) And at the end of the news program, the same anchorwoman invites viewers to see the latest Latin American, Turkish or even Japanese soap opera from Univision, Telemundo or somewhere else—an hour sure to include women being berated, thrown about, slapped and beaten . . . and men whipping out the latest handgun (held sideways, of course) to shoot someone who has offended them somehow.

These violent, antisocial programs are on Monday through Friday, not late at night, but at 7 p.m.! Then the media, as well as civic and religious leaders, wonder aloud where Puerto Rico's domestic violence comes from?! Some even ascribe it to mainland culture. The truth is, successive generations of Puerto Rico's children have been, and continue to be, taught that THIS is how you interact with women if you want to be a man, and THIS is how you settle a score with another man: with violence. You think this programming might have something to do with where the island's kids get their ideas about how to act as grown-ups?

Yes, I do have a bone to pick with the Puerto Rican's mass media. And it affects the destiny of the island and the rest of the United States as well. Owned as they are by the foreign networks that cater to stateside Hispanics (the great majority of them Mexican Americans or Mexican immigrants), the programs they buy and air target that larger group, not the Caribbean Hispanics in the states. The news segments they make available to their stations on the island cover what's going on in Mexico, Central and South America. As a result, the US citizens living in Puerto Rico are better informed about what's going on in Ecuador, Peru and Colombia than they are about what's going on where their children and grandchildren live in the states! But that's what the local news programs here get from their foreign owners, and it's cheaper than doing their own original reporting.

The newspapers, especially the status-quo *El Nuevo Día*, are guilty as well. They place stateside news not under "National" (that refers to Puerto Rico for them) but under "International" news, as if the country that protects them, feeds them and issues their passports were a foreign country. They also refer to President Obama as "*el presidente norteamericano Barack Obama*," as if referring to another country's leader. For the first time, more Puerto Ricans now live in the States than on the island. Yet neither the island's local TV news programs nor the local newspapers dedicate space to what's going on where the other half of the Puerto Rican family lives. Can't these stations here do two minutes of news affecting the diaspora in Orlando, Atlanta, New York or Chicago?

The problem for both the island and the United States is that the media here reinforce the idea that the US citizens of Puerto Rico are not really Americans at all; they are *Latin* Americans. Governor García Padilla came right out and said it in an address to the National Press Club in 2016, during the debt crisis meltdown (emphasis added): "We are Latins that are American citizens. But we are Latins. **Puerto Rico, this is a Latin American country.** And we are very proud of it, and we want to remain Latins."

This ambivalence, or social schizophrenia, reflects the fear of change that pervades the political dialogue today. When I say "fear," I also refer to a fear of rejection: many Puerto Ricans fear that "the United States just doesn't want us." That is directly related to the topic of racial bias and the whole Hispanic controversy of brown versus white in today's United States.

I agree to a point. Puerto Rico is often described in the mainland press as poverty-stricken, debt-ridden, raging with uncontrolled rampant crime, political and police corruption. This could be just as true of many places in the continental United States as well. But it is far from being the complete picture.

Puerto Rico's Status

Rejecting colonialism in any form, the United Nations and international law endorse only three versions of sovereignty: (1) independence; (2) associated republic or (3) statehood within a federated republic. With Puerto Rico's status for the past hundred plus years being described as either a colony or a territory of the United States, only two of those options are currently on the table. But first, more background. The vast majority of Puerto Ricans are Americanized and wish to remain so in some form. Those to the right (conservatives) tend to want statehood. The middle road prefers the status-quo offered by the existing commonwealth status, but this has been harder and harder to maintain since the days of Muñoz Marín and his

"Operation Bootstrap." The economy of the world has shifted, and the current model is clearly obsolete. It's like driving a Model-T on the Autobahn. The Popular Democratic Party (PDP) has proposed a "new and enhanced" commonwealth, but that was rejected in principle by the US government at 2016 hearings held by the House Committee of the Interior for being inconsistent with the US Constitution. This, and the same conclusion in an earlier White House Task Force report, prompted President Barack Obama to call for and for Congress to approve $2.5 million to be set aside to instruct and guide the island's voters as to the "constitutionality prior to a referendum" of any new relationship with the United States, an effort that would be scrutinized by the US Department of Justice.

For four years (2012-16), the status-quo PDP García Padilla administration took no steps toward holding a referendum or plebiscite, despite 54% voting to change the island's relationship to the United States. *No conviene.* Not only that, Governor García Padilla spent millions in island taxpayers' money to hire anti-statehood lobbyists in Washington, DC, even though Congress' position is that 61% voted for the statehood alternative in the 2012 plebiscite; he was fighting the will of the people with their own tax dollars!

The left (liberals) is generally for independence, but because so few voters support the Independence Party, it has been required to be re-certified as a legitimate party with petitions every four years, just to keep it on the ballot. This ideal is embraced and espoused mostly by the artistically and academically inclined, the stuff of the poet and dreamer inside each of us a bit, and some whose families had their immense land holdings broken up and distributed by the Americans one hundred years ago. The impracticality of this option, including the loss of US programs and citizenship, is a major obstacle to the growth of this party now and in the future. I recently read in the press about a new splinter group that has emerged, requesting a return to Spanish rule as a province! That won't go anywhere. Not surprisingly, after 400 years of Spanish rule and speaking Spanish, most Puerto Ricans consider themselves cultural descendants of Spain. Today, however, many tend to identify culturally as part of

Latin America, something conveniently fostered by the island's mostly foreign-owned local media, as discussed earlier.

Another status accepted by the world community is that of "associated republic," and the PPD tends to push this option. The only problems are Puerto Rico would have to vote to become independent first (highly unlikely) and then negotiate a treaty of association with Congress, something that either party could unilaterally declare null and void at any time. Automatic US citizenship by being born on the island would stop, as well as most federal programs and the jurisdiction of federal regulatory agencies (EPA, FDIC, SBA, etc.). With the arrival of shopping malls, cable TV and the internet, each successive generation has become more and more Americanized, and support for statehood has consistently grown, to where in 2012 54% voted to change the current territorial status, with statehood receiving either a majority (61%), if you count votes cast, or a plurality, if you also count votes not cast on that question. Congress made it clear that it only recognizes votes cast, not counting those left blank as being votes "against" anything.

Puerto Rico has been a United States colony since 1898, and I personally believe that we must be granted either statehood or independence, as the colony no longer is viable. The model is old, and we must get on with making certain that the people of Puerto Rico are treated as full citizens: either as their own independent nation or as a state of the Union. In my opinion, the next plebiscite or referendum on the island's status needs to offer only those options that fit within the US Constitution: statehood or independence. Living here now, my choice is easy: full US citizenship and economic development (jobs) that only statehood can provide.

Congress works along the lines of the "art of the deal": trades, compromises, negotiations done among equals, sometimes along party lines but mostly along relational lines. The equals all have one important thing in common: they vote on the floor in Congress. Puerto Rico does not have a vote, so it can't play. The resident commissioner scurries around with a paid mercenary army of employees from his small office and from the Puerto Rico Office of Federal Affairs, which is under the governor's purview. When they belong to the same political party, they work closely together; however, they are often in opposition! They all lobby congressmen, but with nothing to trade. And congressmen have to carefully weigh first and foremost their own constituents' needs. Are they willing to sacrifice that? The answer is mostly NO. And that goes for the four Puerto Ricans who serve in Congress today. They owe themselves first and foremost to Brooklyn, the Bronx, Chicago and Idaho, not to Puerto Rico.

In the history of the United States Congress, there have only been six people of Puerto Rican ancestry who have had a vote on the floor; the US citizens of the island have never had a vote on the floor.

Puerto Rico would benefit greatly from having five to six congressmen (or women) and two senators. The present structure of having one non-voting delegate for the island in reality disenfranchises all 3.5 million Puerto Ricans living on the island. This stagnant, unjust, situation must be remedied.

The Congress that I joined in 1978 had five voting Hispanic members and one resident commissioner who represented Puerto Rico and did not have the authority to vote for passage of legislation. Today there are thirty-five members of Congress of Hispanic descent and another two non-voting members from Puerto Rico and the Mariana Islands (the US Virgin Islands Commissioner is not Hispanic). Based on population projections, the number of Hispanics in Congress will multiply in the years to come. The problems Puerto Rico has been facing would not exist if Puerto Rico were a state with five representatives in the House and two senators.

My friend and former colleague, Congressman Xavier Becerra from California, is often quoted as saying, "The only difference between those of us who share the same Hispanic culture is the color of the beans we eat." He's right. Hispanics in the United States now number 56 million (not counting Puerto Rico's 3.5 million), making it the largest minority in the United States. And the Hispanic population is growing. The median age is twenty-seven years. By 2050 it is expected that Hispanics will be the largest ethnic group in the United States. Today this sector is represented by twenty-nine congressmen and women, as well as three senators. If Puerto Rico were added to the group, with five representatives and two senators, the island would be part of a major voting block that would come into play on issues affecting US Hispanics on the continent and the island. As a founding member and two-term chairman of the Congressional Hispanic Caucus, I can personally attest to the power that represents and what those numbers can achieve. As part of this group, Puerto Rico would have this block of instant allies and a ready-made power structure in place to join forces with. And that doesn't include non-Hispanic members who come from states with significant Hispanic populations. Political clout lies in the number of votes in Congress.

* * *

Puerto Rico as a state of the Union would be a far cry from what it is today. It would be the hub of the Caribbean, a technology-transfer bridge to Latin America and a beacon of democratic principles in the region.

Much of what I read these days seems to assume that under statehood Puerto Rico would have the same present structure of a non-voting member with a tin cup begging for alms from the federal government. This is surely not meant as criticism of the many individuals who have served as resident commissioners when I served in Congress and who were personal friends. Out of courtesy we called them "congressman," but in reality, they are not. A member of Congress is responsible for about 700,000 people in a specified, compact and contiguous area (up from my day when I represented 500,000); but a resident commissioner is expected to serve 3.5 million citizens living in Puerto Rico. Puerto Rico's taxpayers pay $24 million to support the Puerto Rico Federal Affairs Office in Washington, DC. As noted earlier, this office is under the governor's office structurally but collaborates with the resident commissioner's office, especially if they belong to the same party, which is the usual situation. However, in 2012 the voters elected Governor García Padilla (PDP), a status-quo or "enhanced" commonwealth supporter, but Resident Commissioner Pedro Pierluisi (PNP) was a statehood supporter. Their party difference meant the resident commissioner's office received less support than usual from the Federal Affairs Office and actually lobbied against the resident commissioner, Pierluisi, who had received more votes than the governor.

As far as taxes are concerned, currently island residents earning income from the US continent are required to report it and file an annual income tax return with the IRS. Bona fide residents of Puerto Rico do not file with the IRS or pay federal income tax on their Puerto Rico income; that is filed with the Treasury (*Hacienda*) of Puerto Rico and may be higher than the federal income tax would be. For years, anti-statehood forces had used the threat of higher taxes if the island were to become a state. However, those living on the island already pay some comparatively high taxes, including a 6.6% commonwealth tariff on imports, excise taxes on mid-size and luxury cars and a local income tax. But real estate—more Puerto Ricans owned their home than the average of homeowners stateside—was under-appraised even during booms in property values, and real estate taxes have never been used to support schools, parks and the myriad things that property taxes are used for on the continent. Up until recently, there had never been a sales tax—with the exception of a 1% sales tax implemented in the early 2000s by the municipality of Caguas south of San Juan.

It was the prospect of a sales tax, a regressive tax which would hit the poor hardest, that anti-statehooders (the Popular Democratic and the Independence parties) used to instill fear in voters, especially the poor, who tended to support statehood because of the parity in federal programs it would bring. They boldly lied to the people of Puerto Rico, saying statehood would mean a first-ever sales tax, even though there is no national sales tax; some states have one, some don't.

The great irony here is that in 2006, and after shutting down the commonwealth government for several days due to cash-flow (over spending), PDP Governor Aníbal Acevedo Vilá introduced Puerto Rico's first sales tax—not 4% or 5% but 7%—and rammed it through the legislature. His party even orchestrated the bizarre sight of a march on the capitol building, with thousands demanding the imposition of a sales tax. Only in Puerto Rico, folks!

In the end, those who had used the imposition of a sales tax as a reason to oppose statehood turned out to be the ones who actually imposed a sales tax on their people. In 2014, another anti-statehood governor, García Padilla, and his PDP-controlled legislature hiked that 7% sales tax to 11.5%, the highest under the US flag, supposedly to address the island's debt crisis. Even with that astronomical tax, joined by several new gasoline taxes, soft-drink taxes and another ninety new taxes imposed over just a few years, Governor García Padilla decided to stiff Puerto Rico's bondholders, including scores of thousands of them living on the island. His administration even pushed, and the legislature passed, a VAT (Value-Added Tax) to replace the sales tax, something most experts believed: (a) would make the effective taxes paid for goods and services nearly 22%; and (b) should not be implemented in an economy flat on its back, like Puerto Rico's was. The VAT was subsequently rescinded.

By 2016, Governor García Padilla announced that the debt was unpayable. By then, his administration's inability or unwillingness to provide audited financial statements—and the lack of confidence on the part of the bond rating agencies who had reduced Puerto Rico's bonds to "junk"—meant one of two things: (1) either the bondholders would sue and there would be a "humanitarian crisis" on the island when it could not continue to borrow to provide essential services; or (2) Congress would have to provide some protection against bondholder suits to avoid such a crisis. Congress decided to do the latter . . . but at a cost unimaginable to the governor: a first-ever Congressional Fiscal Control Board to "supervise" spending going forward.

How could Congress impose such a control board on the Free-Associated State of Puerto Rico? It certainly could, and did, because over the previous several years all three branches of the federal government had clearly stated that Puerto Rico is still a territory, subject to the plenary power of Congress as provided in the US Constitution—and as even admitted by PDP founder Governor Luis Muñoz Marín in the congressional hearings on the "Commonwealth" of Puerto Rico's 1952 Constitution.

If Puerto Rico were to become a state, all income would be subject to federal taxes, and the law would apply to anyone earning the minimum requirement under the federal laws. The commonwealth could opt to do what some of the states have done: eliminate the state income taxes, as Florida has, and downsize several agencies. In any case, it would require a complete revision of the local tax system and the local government structure, something which will happen before statehood as a result of the island's debt crisis and Congress' imposition of the Fiscal Control Board in September 2016.

Is English-only a prerequisite for statehood? As far as I know, neither the Constitution of United States nor any state's constitution establishes an "official" language for the government. Nor was the adoption of such a "language law" ever imposed on a territory as a condition for admission to the Union. In fact, there were more Spanish-speakers than English-speakers in many of the territories when they applied for statehood. Why, the very names of many of our states are Spanish words! Colorado. Florida. Nevada. Montana. California. Arizona. There are great metro areas today where more Spanish is spoken than English. Should those areas be exempt from an English-only requirement imposed on Puerto Rico?

The idea that Spanish will replace English in the United States and that adding a predominantly Spanish-speaking Puerto Rico as the 51st state will only accelerate the process is simply not borne out by the facts. First, Puerto Rico is increasingly bilingual and, since laws passed in 2012 some public schools are implementing English as the language of instruction. Second, the Pew Research Center projects that the number of Hispanic Spanish-only speakers in the United States will actually decline in the years ahead, and that Hispanic English-only speakers will increase as successive generations of Hispanics adopt English as their first language. And third, what about the many billions of dollars that stateside taxpayers have spent over the past seven-plus decades teaching kids Spanish in high school? The United States is suddenly afraid of Spanish? Please! If America is to remain the world's leading economy, it's not only going to need Spanish-speakers, but Chinese-speakers as well.

Conventional wisdom and the press hold that a local election for Congress in Puerto Rico would result in only Democrats being elected. We'd do well to remember another bit of conventional wisdom: people expected Hawaii to elect Republicans and Alaska to elect Democrats when they were admitted to the Union in 1959. The electorate voted exactly the opposite: Hawaii elected Democrats and Alaska elected Republicans. So much for conventional wisdom. Then consider that Puerto Ricans are socially conservative and are closer to the Republican position on LGBTQ+ rights, abortion, the legalization of drugs, crime, etc.

The founder of the pro-statehood party, Luis A. Ferré, was a Republican and active in the GOP at the national committee level. The governor immediately prior to García Padilla, Luis Fortuño, was a Republican elected in a true landslide by the voters of Puerto Rico in 2008, and in November 2016, Republican Jennifer González was elected resident commissioner. Republicans holding the House and gaining control of both the White House and the Senate in the 2016 general elections were all good things for statehood's prospects. Ironically, statehood for Puerto Rico has been in the GOP platform for decades, with Presidents Ford and Bush calling for it during State of the Union addresses, while the Democrats have been ambiguous at best so as not to offend the island's status-quo PDP and liberal independence supporters on the mainland who tend to vote Democratic.

It is my opinion that if today's extreme right-leaning Republican Congress had to vote on the 1917 Jones Act that granted US citizenship to Puerto Ricans, it wouldn't pass in the existing anti-Hispanic, anti-immigrant climate. It will take a monumental amount of education and pressure from the Puerto Rican diaspora in the states and in the Congressional Hispanic Caucus to move the needle. On the other hand, following the upset victory of Donald Trump and the Republican Party, they both know that the nation's demographics are not on their side in the next several decades and that they will need to treat their Hispanic citizens the same as all other US citizens if they hope to win control again.

Puerto Ricans are not immigrants. They are US citizens living in a political condition that would be intolerable for any other US citizen. The US Government Accountability office study struck down the long-held myth that it would cost the Treasury too much to admit Puerto Rico into the Union. How do you prorate the value of even one US citizen, let alone 3.5 million of them? No matter what US state they were born in, once they move and become bona fide residents of Puerto Rico, they lose their right to vote for the Congress or for the President. If they had moved to a foreign country, living under a foreign flag, they would still be able to vote by absentee ballot.

Does this make any sense? Does it represent justice in any way? It doesn't to me.

Epilogue

by Jane Lee Garcia

January 2018

Although this book was twelve years in the writing, the Epilogue was still unfinished when Bob went into the VA Hospital in San Juan, Puerto Rico in December, 2016 . . . and passed away from COPD-related complications on January 25, 2017.

In the weeks following his passing, he was honored by the Senate of Puerto Rico with lying-in-state at the Capitol; by a Proclamation and Observance by the New York State Senate; by his father's church in the Bronx; by the US House of Representatives in a Memorial Observance and in the Congressional Record; by the Congressional Hispanic Caucus and Institute; and by his country with the internment of his remains at Arlington National Cemetery.

It took me almost a year to bring myself to write this on his behalf, using verbatim transcripts of Bob's recordings and handwritten notes.

We spent the last years of Bob's life together . . . 24/7/365 . . . in many ways for the very first time. In public life you don't have much of an opportunity to live for self. We had no regrets; we were both thrilled to serve, loved every minute of it and were dedicated to those who had elected and reelected Bob, and even to those who hadn't. We had the privilege of making a difference in many people's lives. Bob loved his Bronx community, something that was evident in the way people loved him back and something I learned over and over again on its streets with him during political campaigns. He also loved the island of his parents and grandparents, the US Territory of Puerto Rico and its 3.5 million people, whom he also served as their only *de facto* voting representative in Congress. We undertook official duties and were given opportunities we had never imagined. And as the parents of a blended family of six offspring and sixteen grandchildren, there were always other family priorities or emergencies to be dealt with. That doesn't mean Bob didn't have periods of deep inward reflection on what he might have done differently . . . or better . . . in his past.

Most of this book's basic text was written during our years in Middelburg, Virginia, from 2004 to 2012. From the very beginning I refused to be his co-author, something I had done or directed in most of public life after our marriage in 1979. I had two reasons. First, I wanted it to be Bob's words, and try as I might to avoid imposing my personality, I would have influenced what ended up being written; it would have been a joint book. But that was not the intention, even though a good portion of the experiences recounted here were lived jointly. We both agreed that this was to be written for those wanting to understand how a kid from the Bronx became a leader both of his local community and an important part of New York State, as well as growing into a national leader who unified and helped launch the Hispanic empowerment movement. It is an American Dream story. It could only happen in America. The second reason was purely selfish; portions of this story pertaining to Wedtech were too upsetting for me to relive. The experience continued to make me angry and had sorely tested my Christian faith regarding the fundamental teachings of Justice and Truth. For this reason, we asked a good friend and published historian, author Dr. Loretta Córdova, to work with Bob directly and privately. Bob would prepare his notes and twice a week would drive to Chantilly, Virginia, where they would spend the day, more or less, shaping it into a narrative. When we left Middleburg, they had a working draft that still needed a lot of work filling in personal details and things that needed to be researched for accuracy.

After moving to Puerto Rico for Bob's health in 2012, we had the good fortune to work with Nick Karahalios, who was Senior

Vice President and Director of Marketing and Business Development for Casiano Communications and its flagship weekly, *Caribbean Business*, founded and run by an old Bronx friend of Bob's: publisher Manuel Casiano. Bob and Manny went way back to long years in New York and were good friends. It was Manny who suggested, actually invited, Bob to make his Puerto Rico office at his company's offices; from this happy coincidence evolved the friendship and trust in Nick that led to his finishing and structuring the manuscript that was ultimately submitted to Hunter College's Department of Puerto Rican Studies for pre-publishing editing in the Spring of 2017. Bob and I had been adamant about offering this historical document to the college for publishing, since all of Bob's official papers and documents from his twenty-five years of public service, both as an assemblyman and then as state senator to his election and years in Congress, had been entrusted to Hunter College when Bob retired in 1990. But Hunter's Centro insisted that they remove Bob's opinions about Puerto Rico's future status, which is not something to be done to anyone's autobiography. We are pleased that Arte Público Press realized the importance of Bob's story and agreed to publish it just as Bob wanted it published.

Our last five years together in Puerto Rico were mostly about us, both individually and together. These invaluable years were the apex and culmination of it all: a final time to really enjoy each other intimately. It made up for, and made sense of, all the past hectic years. I would wish this kind of experience for everyone: to embrace it, understand it and appreciate more than anything what it means to have that one special person to share it with. That can only come from having shared your life fully.

Most of this Epilogue was written at Bob's request in the autumn of 2016 as he mused aloud to me every day at our morning times together, and more expansively watching spectacular sunsets as we sat on our terrace overlooking Old San Juan and San Juan Bay. All the while he continued, as health permitted, working together with Nick on the details of his book, chapter by chapter. He was tempted to include more and more, as his thoughts were triggered by the review process. It took an experienced hand to guide him through this phase. Nick "got" Bob, and I am ever grateful that he was able to be that guide.

The unexpected benefit that moving to Puerto Rico had for Bob was a more realistic understanding of the people and land his parents had left in 1924. It was "mind-blowing," as Bob had only visited the island periodically his whole life: first to visit family, later on for official visits. As a born and bred New Yorker, he identified with the Puerto Rican community his parents had left behind, in many ways a source of pure rapture as he visited the island's breathtaking interior and the many towns he had never seen, absorbing the natural beauty and the wonderful people and foods he was instinctively drawn to from his childhood memories. He had loved Puerto Rico all his life, as many in the diaspora have: an ideal left behind. Now he was coming to love it as a Puerto Rican, seen from this new perspective.

As Bob wrote,

> Having dedicated 25 of my years on Earth to public service, I can think of no higher calling or mission in life. I am a product of a government that worked. I went to public schools, served in the US Army acquiring a skill in electronics and finished studies on a GI Bill. The government is not a business. The difference is huge: business works to produce a profit; government functions to serve and protect its people. They are different as night and day. I love the people of the South Bronx who gave me the opportunity to serve, first as a New York state assemblyman, a state senator and finally as a US congressman. The happiest moments of my life were walking the streets of my community, talking to the hard-working folks that looked to me to make things fairer and improve their chances of realizing the American Dream. Many times, people just want to know somebody cares enough to listen to them. I did and I still do. Loving people and listening are the best qualifications for public office. Next is education.
>
> In late 2012, after another bout of pneumonia, my doctors advised me to change climates due to advanced pulmonary disease. After a cursory review of the Earth's warmer zones, Jane and I decided to move to Puerto Rico. Although I have visited the island since my twenties on a regular basis, sometimes several times a year,

living there was not something I had ever thought of. Without further ado, we disposed of three quarters of our belongings and in March of 2013 we arrived courtesy of the Bronx-based moving company Rosa del Monte (who had moved us several times before) at our new forever home in front of Parque Muñoz Rivera on La Isleta de San Juan, Puerta de Tierra.

Once living on the island where his parents (and I) had been born, he was appalled at the pervasive poverty and ignorance in which so many still lived "in the twenty-first century!" The island's rural interior was a step back in time. People rode horses to the local *colmadito*, or store—how very quaint. *Campesinos* loaded *calabazas* and plantains onto old trucks to get them to market. Children frolicked barefoot with wide-staring eyes. Oxen plowed furrows in the rich volcanic earth. Paradise on earth.

Many people in Puerto Rico feel that this is ideal, retaining our "culture" and "old ways." So did Bob. At first.

As part of the Puerto Rican diaspora, I, like many, held Puerto Rico in my heart as an ideal, a starting or reference point that gave me a place to be from. As an official and politician with a constituency that was fluid in movement back and forth from the island to the Bronx, I kept in touch with the needs and demands for equal governmental treatment in Puerto Rico. I felt it was part of my job both in New York and when I later was able to include Puerto Rico in many legislative measures that gave them equal footing in many benefits that as US citizens they were entitled to.

His daily reading of the newspapers left him increasingly frustrated and wishing he was still in Congress. He was mystified by the media referring to Puerto Rico as a "country" or *país* in both English and Spanish-language news reports. He would say "What 'country', *qué 'país'*? Don't people here on this island realize this isn't a separate country?"

When we visited the island's schools, he was dismayed by the lack of emphasis on core subjects, and particularly the lack of English, math and science teachers. He compared the public-school curriculum to his visits to the 115-year-old private Robinson School in

San Juan and the Residential Center of Educational Opportunities (CROEM) in Mayagüez, a sort of public charter school for the above-average. He then started taking his own (unscientific) private survey, questioning supermarket check-out people, Walmart pharmacy employees, students, maintenance workers in our buildings, public employees and taxi drivers on their knowledge and learning of English. Most, if not all, who spoke good English had lived in the States! The others went to private or parochial school. He began to fret about a population divided both culturally and economically. This wasn't a matter of status to him, but of equal opportunity.

Having traveled the world as a congressman and US representative to NATO, he'd seen the importance of English as the world's language of banking, commerce, arts, music and medicine. He wondered what reasoning could possibly be behind the island's uncompetitive educational policies, particularly since (as part of the United States) assistance was available. Official reports in the newspapers on the physical deterioration of schools, lack of teachers to fill vacancies, misappropriations of federal funds, the reticence or failure of Puerto Rico's authorities to even apply for Head Start and other programs for which Puerto Rico was qualified truly pained him . . . because he could do nothing about it.

My first discovery was that although people in the professional classes spoke good English, many in working or service classes did not or were afraid to. Upon calling any government agency, if you pressed the number for English on your dial, you could wait all day for someone to answer. If you called and spoke English, they sometimes had to find someone to speak to you or would just hang up. In fact, many service businesses were not much better. Particularly annoying was the dominant cable company whose call center was in the Dominican Republic. The English spoken there is also a bit culturally different from Puerto Rican English, which is a more Americanized way of expression.

I made it a point over the next few years to ask people where they learned to speak English, if I couldn't spot them as having either lived in the States or served in the military. Every single one that spoke good English had been taught in private or parochial schools.

Not one from public schools spoke English easily, if at all! That includes graduates from the UPR and some other college-level schools. Those that did speak had paid for special language courses, but most couldn't afford it. I cannot but conclude that this is a systematic erosion of knowledge that divides Puerto Ricans into those with an opportunity and future of higher paying jobs as well as ability to live anywhere in the US mainland and work. Those denied basic English as it was taught in the past in elementary through high school are denied advancement. Both my parents had eighth-grade educations in the first decades of the twentieth century that included normal English subjects and grammar, and upon arrival in New York in 1924, they were instantly employable.

Today, only conversational English is taught in high school as a language, and even at the college level. What advantage does this give our US citizens from Puerto Rico? Those that left in the last emigration in recent years were mainly professionals who spoke English well enough to get good jobs. In speaking to a lot of these people, the main reason to relocate was because they wanted a better education for their own kids.

Personal security and better-paying jobs are also strong reasons to leave an island where public services have spiraled downward. Countries in this hemisphere such as Ecuador, Peru, Chile and Colombia have all instituted programs to teach English to their students, including at the primary and secondary levels, because even those governments, some that aren't particularly friendly to the United States, recognize the importance of having their own citizens competitive in the world markets.

Meanwhile in the last couple of decades in Puerto Rico, the same political leaders of separatists or pro-colonial parties who dismantled English-language teaching in the public schools also managed to send their own children to the private schools taught in English, this at the same time that those same elected official were denying the children of the working poor that competitive edge in life. This is a gross injustice that should be corrected at once to give our citizens back one of the major advantages they have as part of being US citizens.

But those who live in the US mainland and have full voting rights are now able to use their clout to bring attention to the fact that under the present colonial arrangement, the island and its residents are in a legal limbo of non-status, and we are currently the after-

thought of the afterthought. Any red-blooded American citizen who moves to the US territory of Puerto Rico loses his or her full constitutional rights as citizens, once they become island residents. Under the American flag this is unprecedented, and we must seek redress for the 3.5 million US citizens who not only don't vote for their own president but also have no representation or votes in the Congress and get only 70% of their Social Security and no COLA!

Every government agency has treated Puerto Rico differently. We have fewer federal allocations, less medical and health funding. We also don't pay federal taxes. Those citizens who do not wish to be a part of the federation of the United States of America need to be counted as well. Then there are the hypocrites. It is very easy for someone living under full US citizenship protections in a country under its rule of law to shout, "¡Viva Puerto Rico Libre!" as I did as a young firebrand starting my political life, to the applause of an emotional public yearning for their warm island home. Yet it would be something else for those same folks to go live in the Republic of Puerto Rico should that ever be the result of a status referendum. Few, if any, Puerto Ricans in the diaspora would do so. And not one would want to go through Customs without a US passport to visit the homeland or relatives in a foreign country.

As I gave thought to this more and more apparent inequality experienced in the island—now my home, although we had not yet declared ourselves legal residents—with the upcoming 2016 elections, we both began to think seriously about the future of Puerto Rico. We were now invested here and the process of registering to vote in the primary elections was almost at the end, when we both decided to do our civic duty by voting where we were now living. To me this was a momentous decision, due to the high value the right to vote was to me personally, especially as a product of the Voting Rights Act. To me the vote is a sacred duty. I also realized that by registering in Puerto Rico, we would both lose our full rights as US citizens and become second-class citizens in the only place in America this double standard exists.

We talked of little else. Then we went into the registry a week before the registration period ended, and that was that. To me in particular this was a statement I had to make. Thus, in 2016 we both voted in the US presidential primary to elect delegates to the Democratic Party Convention and the territory's governor and leg-

islature, which in Puerto Rico are elected every four years during the presidential election in November.

Bob was a lover of history and wanted to understand how Puerto Rico came to its present dilemma. He began to delve ever deeper into the early relationship between the federal government and its new possession at the beginning of the twentieth century, especially as it affected US citizenship and the rights it extended or did not.

For the life of me I cannot understand how the US government in the 1917 Jones Act created millions of American citizens on a piece of Caribbean-island real estate then left them in limbo! Some writers or so-called experts have alluded to the United States' need for Puerto Rico's young men as "cannon fodder" in the First World War as the reason for extending US citizenship, but the more I read in well-researched analysis, this was not the case. America's latent racism held that all non-whites made inferior fighting men, and in fact Puerto Ricans did not see meaningful combat but were assigned to support units.

Other writers hold that US citizenship was extended or imposed, based on their view of America, to blunt any pro-independence sentiment and give the Monroe Doctrine a tangible outpost in the Caribbean. But for me, in view of the island's abject economic situation after 400 years as a Spanish colony, one that decades later would still have Puerto Rico called "the poorhouse of the Caribbean," it was the economic prospects facing the island at that time that had its young men seeking a better life, and like adventuresome young men everywhere, they answered the call.

Even on this there are conflicting views that need to be sorted out by historians, but as recorded in Our New Possessions (1898), by Trumball White, an eyewitness freelance reporter present at the transfer of power from Spain to the US in 1898, for the young men lined up to volunteer for the US Army at the old post office in San Juan during World War I, it meant escape from the grinding poverty. In the end, many thousands reported for induction, but only 20,000 were ultimately accepted. Lack of English proficiency, as well as bad health due to pervasive malnutrition and diseases, such as parasites, dysentery, malaria and tuberculosis, kept many from being enlisted.

Puerto Rican soldiers, sailors, pilots and Marines have also served with distinction in every war since. Today, Puerto Rico no longer has a major US military presence on the island, such as the giant Naval base at Roosevelt Roads, Ramey Air Field and the Navy installations in San Juan or Army facilities at Ft. Buchanan; all were once a part of the United States' geopolitical strategy to protect the Panama Canal and regional US interests. However, having the island as an outpost of the American flag in the Caribbean, the supposed "crossroads of the Americas," can still be advantageous to the United States in the twenty-first century and for the future of Puerto Rico as part of many other strategies for both economic and political advantage to the United States.

Besides revamping the tourist business and redeveloping the ports of Roosevelt Roads and Ponce as well as San Juan for maximum benefit to tourism, manufacturing and trade in the hemisphere, Puerto Rico can and should be positioned as the natural energy hub by developing the Caribbean Undersea Energy Cable Grid, an energy network linking the region in sustainable and renewable energy as the basis for a new trade and economic development leadership that would make us a valuable asset to our country as well as the proud, new fifty-first state.

In the words of the first Puerto Rican elected as governor in 1948, Luis Muñoz Marín, "No somos pro americanos; somos americanos. No nos cobija la ciudadanía americana; lo llevamos dentro. Creo que nuestra función es enriquecer la Unión americana con nuestra presencia y no meramente agregarle un pedazo de similitud a la Unión americana." ("We are not pro-American; we are Americans. American citizenship is not something we wear, but something we carry within us. I believe our purpose is to enrich the American Union with our presence and not be just another piece of it.")

"Where are all the billions in federal assistance going?" Bob would ask me every time we drove to the Veterans Administration Hospital, bouncing over a well-used highway full of dangerous, axle-bending craters . . . right in the Metro area. He wondered about it aloud to Nick every time he drove down Fernández Juncos Avenue, a major artery in the capital that cuts through the Santurce area of San Juan on the way to his office at Casiano's. Then he'd read in the newspapers that the island's Highway and Transportation Department was underfunded, had no money and was in debt to the hilt, but the newspapers gave no valid reasons for the federal money being unavailable—one reason is Puerto Rico's insistence on 18 instead of 21 as the minimum age for drinking, making it ineligible for considerable federal highway funds.

Bob spoke to many local government officials, including some of the mayors of larger towns, asking if they needed his help in the application process or a push from above, if their application had been submitted and was pending. He received only one response, from the mayor of a town on the west coast: "Could you help get us funding for an amusement complex?" I won't repeat his response!

These factors and too many others to mention were a big disappointment as he came to understand that Puerto Rico was digging a hole for itself that it could never get out of. He felt he could have/should have done more, insisted more, when he was in Congress, not only within Congress but with the island's government officials in power at the time. They didn't understand the process, and he could have been more helpful.

I am grateful that Bob didn't have to live through Hurricanes Irma and María in September 2017. First, because of the inconsistent electric power provided by the Puerto Rico Electric Power Authority, the government-run monopoly, even before those back-to-back hurricanes wreaked havoc on the fragile (due to deferred maintenance of its distribution grid) electric system. His increasing need for oxygen support would have put him, and thousands equally ill, in life-or-death situations. But even worse would have been for him to witness post-hurricane Puerto Rico. I don't mean the physical devastation in the wake of a terrifying natural disaster. I mean the uncovering of the hidden truth of the abandonment and wretchedness Puerto Rico has been undergoing for decades. Average people in Puerto Rico hadn't fully understood that abysmal poverty, children without teachers and developmental programs, poor medical services, the escalation of abuse of minors and domestic violence denoted a societal descent into hopelessness. People had been leaving Puerto Rico for the mainland in droves (an estimated 400,000) during the previous four years alone in search of better schooling, better medical services and better jobs as all these things deteriorated. It was not just because of the lack of federal funding, but also because of corruption and the lack of creative economic management. In short, the productive people, who are able to flee the Island of Enchantment are resettling in the Land of Opportunity.

Bob often spoke to me while still in Congress in the 1980s to bemoan the gross ignorance of too many members of Congress regarding Puerto Rico. He spent so much time educating his colleagues that he earned the title of Mr. Puerto Rico. It was a source of constant amazement to him that these "leaders of the world" lacked such basic information and yet voted on legislation that affected millions of US citizens. Many didn't even know Puerto Ricans were US citizens or even where it was located, or that it was a part of the United States and that we used the same postal and monetary systems. He often encountered this in federal agencies, as a constant flow of Puerto Rican government officials, bankers and merchants came to his office seeking redress for unfair treatment. He would say, "The truth of the matter is that Puerto Rico is the afterthought of the afterthought!" Or other times he would tell me, "Puerto Rico suffers from 'Benign Neglect'"—the term used to describe putting America's racial problems "on the back burner." On the other hand, he was appalled at the lack of an effective understanding of how to get things done in Washington, DC that prevailed within the local government. Not much has changed on that topic, even today, except now we have been in the news constantly for all our accumulated debt and deficiencies.

In sum, this is not so much about politics as public service. Bob really attributed all the island's ills to the revolving patronage system, which has approximately 30% of the workforce employed by the government at some level. In addition to a bloated central bureaucracy, there are seventy-eight municipalities (seventy-eight mayors, vice mayors, assistants to the mayors, *et al.*) for just 3.4 million people! He blamed a system where there was no Civil Service and where, in every four-year-election cycle, generally unqualified political organizers got positions in the post-election government bureaucracy. More often than not, educational preparation for these jobs in public administration was not required nor ever enforced in this "winner take all," "spoils of war" tradition. Bob saw this as leading to rampant cronyism, nepotism and party allegiance above the common good.

There is a huge difference between a public employee and a public servant. Bob tried writing about the importance of a Civil Service in the opinion section of the English-language newspapers but got no public response or official reaction. Nothing can ever change in Puerto Rico, if this fundamental insurance of a functioning, stable democratic government, staffed by qualified non-political professionals, is not addressed.

Bob was once described by a writer of the *Washington Post* as "bordering on bruiser," not just referring to his size or stance but to his willingness to take on and fight for a righteous cause. If he felt the cause was right, he would lead the charge. Much of his career was dedicated to righting wrongs, helping the poor gain a foothold on a leveled playing field, fighting discrimination, bringing criminal justice reform, promoting equality in education and standing up for immigrants, who fed and nurtured the creativity of this nation.

He was, first and foremost, an American who put his life on the line for his country and was proud of it. He was a Puerto Rican by his parentage and always identified himself as such by association and sentiment. Most of all, Bob loved; he loved all people, he loved the Bronx, he loved New York, he loved God and his family and he loved me. He approached life that way, lived it fully, took the good with the bad and made the best of it, seeking the opportunity to improve, learn and go on.

Bob Garcia was a great man. He was both a good man and a good guy . . . or as his parents and all who knew him would have said, *Gente buena y buena gente*.

Among his parting words are these:

> As I have enjoyed my last years overlooking the Atlantic and San Juan Harbor from my lofty perch, I always wonder what will become of this beautiful island and its wonderful people. I have the optimistic hope that the new generations of leaders, both in Puerto Rico and the continental United States, will ultimately seek what is best for the people.

Index